A

SERIES OF PLANS

FOR

COTTAGES OR HABITATIONS

OF THE

LABOURER,

EITHER IN

HUSBANDRY, OR THE MECHANIC ARTS,

ADAPTED AS WELL TO TOWNS AS TO THE COUNTRY.

ENGRAVED ON THIRTY PLATES.

TO WHICH IS ADDED

An Introduction, containing many useful Observations on this Class of Building; tending to the Comfort of the Poor and Advantage of the Builder: with Calculations of Expences.

BY THE LATE

Mr. J. WOOD, of Bath, Architect.

A NEW EDITION,

CORRECTED TO THE PRESENT TIME.

LONDON:

PRINTED FOR J. TAYLOR, AT THE ARCHITECTURAL LIBRARY, No. 59, HIGH HOLBORN.

1806.

ISBN 0 576 15177 7
Republished in 1972 by Gregg International Publishers Limited
Westmead, Farnborough, Hants., England.

Printed in Offset by Kingprint Limited
Richmond, Surrey, England.

INTRODUCTION.

SOME time back when in company with several gentlemen of landed property, the converfation turned on the ruinous ftate of the cottages of this kingdom; it was obferved that thefe habitations of that ufeful and neceffary rank of men, the LABOURERS, were become for the moft part offenfive both to decency and humanity; that the ftate of them and how far they might be rendered more comfortable to the poor inhabitants, was a matter worthy the attention of every man of property not only in the country, but in large villages, in towns, and in cities.

Reflecting on this converfation; recollecting that no architect had, as yet, thought it worth his while to offer to the publick any well conftructed plans for cottages; confidering the regular gradation between the plan of the moft fimple hut and that of the moft fuperb palace; that a palace is nothing more than a cottage IMPROVED; and that the plan of the latter is the bafis as it were of plans for the former; prompted alfo by humanity to make my talent ufeful to the pooreft of my fellow citizens; I refolved on turning my thoughts towards an object of fuch importance to the publick as plans for cottages appeared to me to be. But in order to make myfelf mafter of the fubject, it was neceffary for me to feel as the cottager himfelf; for I have always

held it as a maxim, and however quaint the thought may appear, yet it is altogether true, that no architect can form a convenient plan, unlefs he ideally places himfelf in the fituation of the perfon for whom he defigns: I fay it was neceffary for me to feel as the cottager himfelf; and for that end to vifit him; to enquire after the conveniencies he wanted, and into the inconveniencies he laboured under.

I did fo; and the further I examined the wider was the field of ftudy that opened itfelf to my view. The neceffity there was of improving the dwellings of the poor labourer became continually more and more apparent. I found it neceffary not to confine myfelf to the habitations of the labourer in hufbandry only, but to confider thofe of the workmen and artificers in the cloathing and other manufacturing counties. I began to be difpirited; to doubt my abilities; and to wifh that a man of greater eminence than myfelf had undertaken fo ufeful a work; a work not unworthy the attention of the moft experienced architect. However I determined to proceed, flattering myfelf, that although I should not produce a perfect work, yet, at the leaft, I fhould lead the way to fome greater improvement.

The greateft part of the cottages that fell

within my observation, I found to be shattered, dirty, inconvenient, miserable hovels, scarcely affording a shelter for beasts of the forest; much less were they proper habitations for the human species; nay it is impossible to describe the miserable condition of the poor cottager, of which I was too often the melancholy spectator.

Of the better kind of these cottages the poor inhabitants complained,

That they were *wet and damp*, from their being built against banks, or in low *dreary* spots; and from the floors of them being sunk, as it were, into the ground, having one step [a] down into them and sometimes two.

That they were *cold and cheerless*, from the entrances not being skreened; from the awkward situation of the door, windows, and chimney; and from the thinness of the external [b] walls.

That they were *inconvenient* from their want of room; and from the steepness, straitness and bad [c] situation of the stairs, where there was an upper floor.

That they were *unhealthy* from the lowness and closeness of the rooms; from their facing mostly the north and west; and from the chambers being crowded into the roof, where having nothing to defend them from the weather but the rafters and bare roof without ceiling, they were stifling hot in the summer, and freezing cold in the winter; the triangular shape of the roof rendered them also incommodious; the dormer windows [d] being continually out of repair, and the dormers leaky, added greatly to the dampness, unhealthiness, and decay of the cottage.

Now to obviate these complaints, and to remove these inconveniencies, I shall lay down the SEVEN following principles, on which all cottages should be built.

First, The cottage should be DRY and HEALTHY; this is effected by keeping the

---

[a] This error is not confined to cottages only, but it is to be observed in most houses in the country; as well in those erected years ago, as in those, strange to say it, built in modern times.

[b] In my neighbourhood they build the external walls, both of cottages and houses, with freestone, barely six inches thick; and in the countries, where brick is made use of, and particularly where the brick is rather dear, I observed they generally made the external walls nine inches, or one brick thick. In the first case I have been often an eye witness of the rain driving, not only through the joints, but even the stone itself; and in the winter, I have seen the inside of these walls covered with ice from the roof to the foundation. In the second case, the same circumstances attend the nine inch walls, as I was informed by the several inhabitants.

[c] The situation of the stairs being generally at the side of the chimney, I need not expatiate on the inconveniency thereby produced; and to the old, and infirm, the steepness or straitness is very troublesome, and dangerous.

[d] Dormer, or dormant windows are such as are commonly placed in the roof; the rafter, on which the cheek or side of the window rests, is called the dormant rafter; and it is easily conceived, how difficult it must be to make the joining betwixt the upright cheek and the tile, or other covering, so close as to prevent leakage, which must of course rot the dormant rafter, and bring on in a short space of time the decay of the roof.

floor *sixteen* or *eighteen* inches [e] above the natural ground; by building it clear of banks, on an open spot of ground, that has a declivity, or fall, from the building; by having the rooms not less than *eight* feet high, an height that will keep them airy and healthy; and by avoiding having chambers in the roof.

Secondly, WARM, CHEERFUL, and COMFORTABLE. In order to attain these points the walls should be of a sufficient thickness (if of stone, not less than *sixteen* inches; if of brick, at least a brick and half;) to keep out the cold of the winter, and the excessive heat of the summer. The entrance should be [f] skreened, that the room, on opening the door, may not be exposed to the open air; the rooms should receive the light from the east, or the [g] south, or from any point betwixt the east and the south; for if they receive their light from the north, they will be cold and cheerless; if from the west, they will be so heated by the summer's afternoon sun, as to become comfortless to the poor labourer after an hard day's work; whereas on the contrary, receiving the light from the east or the south, they will be always warm and cheerful; so like the feelings of men in an higher sphere are those of the poor cottager, that if his habitation be warm, cheerful, and comfortable, he will return to it with gladness, and abide in it with pleasure.

Thirdly, CONVENIENT, by having a porch, or shed, to skreen the entrance and to hold the labourers tools; by having a shed to serve as a pantry, and store-place for fuel; by having a privy [h] for cleanliness and decency's sake; by a proper disposition of the windows doors, and chimneys; by having the stairs, where there is an upper floor, not less than *three feet* wide; the rise, or height not more than *eight inches*, and the tread, or breadth not less than *nine inches;* and lastly by proportioning the size of the cottage to the family that is to inhabit it; there should be

---

[e] For want of this precaution, I have always observed, that in wet summers, and throughout the whole winter, the walls sucked up (if I may be allowed the expression) the water, and are damp for at least a yard high; and this happens not only where the walls are thin, but even in buildings where they are thick.

[f] This circumstance must be particularly attended to, in those rooms where there is intended to be a bed.

[g] At first view this nicety may appear trifling, but on mature deliberation will prove of very material consequence.

[h] This convenience will answer many good ends, but in nothing more than being an *introduction to cleanliness.* In the account of the voyage to the South Sea, published by Dr. Hawksworth, speaking of the inhabitants of New Zealand is the following passage. " In personal delicacy they were not equal to our friends at Otaheite, for the coldness of the climate " did not so often invite them to bathe, but we saw among them one instance of cleanliness, in which they excelled them, " and of which perhaps there is no example in any other Indian Nation; every house or every cluster of three or four " houses was furnished with a *privy*, so that the ground was every where clean." What a reflection is this on the greatest part of the inhabitants of Britain to be exceeded in neatness in any one point by that barbarous race of people the New Zealanders? I could mention many large and opulent towns, particularly on the sea coasts, nay some large cities, where there is scarcely such a convenience in the whole place, for want of which, the streets are perfect jakes; to the annoyance of both Inhabitants and Strangers.

one lodging room for the parents, another for the female, and a third for the male children; it is melancholy to fee a man and his wife, and fometimes half a dozen children crowded together in the fame room, nay often in the fame bed; the horror is ftill heightened, and the inconveniency increafed at the time when the woman is in child-bed, or in cafe of illnefs, or of death; indeed whilft the children are young, under nine years of age, there is not that offence to decency if they fleep in the fame room with their parents, or if the boys and girls fleep together, but after that age they fhould be kept [i] apart.

Fourthly, Cottages fhould not be more than TWELVE feet wide in the clear [k] being the greateft width that it would be prudent to venture the rafters of the roof with the collar pieces [l] *only*, without danger of fpreading the walls; and by ufing collar pieces, there can be fifteen inches in height of the roof thrown into the upper chambers, which will render dormer windows [m] ufelefs. The collar pieces will ferve for ceiling joifts; and the fmall portion of the roof, that is thrown into the room, will not create thofe inconveniencies that attend rooms, which are totally in the roof.

Fifthly, Cottages fhould be always built in PAIRS; either at a little diftance the one from the other; or clofe adjoining fo as to appear as one building, that the inhabitants may be of affiftance to each other in cafe of ficknefs or any other accident.

Sixthly, As a piece of OECONOMY, cottages fhould be built ftrong, and with the beft of materials, and thefe materials well put together; the mortar muft be well tempered and mixt, and lime not fpared; hollow walls bring on decay, and harbour vermin; and bad fappy timber foon reduces the cottage to a ruinous ftate; although I would by no means

[i] I am aware that the ftatute of the 5th of Elizabeth, concerning the apprenticing poor children, and compelling adults to go out to fervice, will be here objected to me, but the objection foon vanifhes when we confider; *firft*, That it may be policy, in many cafes, to let the children live at home with their parents 'till they are grown up, particularly in the manufacturing Countries; where the trade of the Father will be more carefully taught the children, whofe earnings often, nay generally, contribute to the better maintenance of the Family. *Secondly*, The power given to the parifh officers by that act is very much circumfcribed, and is confined merely to their own parifhes; indeed they may, if they can find proper mafters in other parifhes, bind out their orphan poor, and the children of fuch poor as are willing to part with them; but this muft be done by the confent of the magiftrates, who fhould be very careful how they take the burthen off from one parifh, and lay it on another.

[k] Twelve feet is a width fufficient for a dwelling that is to be deemed a cottage; if it be wider, it approaches too near to what I would call a houfe for a fuperior tradefman; befides, it would require longer and ftronger timbers, girders to the floors and roof, and confequently greatly enhance the expence; a circumftance one would wifh in all buildings to avoid.

[l] A collar piece, is that piece of wood which ties the rafters together at fome height above the wall plate, as is expreffed in Fig. 1. in the firft mifcellaneous plate, by the letter A. and is generally dove-tailed into the rafters.

[m] Becaufe the room being *fix feet ten inches* high to the top of the wall plate, there will be fufficient height to make a window in the fide wall under the plate.

have thefe cottages fine, yet I recommend regularity, which is beauty; regularity will render them ornaments to the country, inftead of their being as at prefent difagreeable objects.

Seventhly, A PIECE OF GROUND for a garden fhould be allotted to every cottage [n] proportionable to its fize; the cottage fhould be built in the vicinity of a fpring of water, a circumftance to be much attended to; and if there be no fpring, let there be a well.

On the foregoing SEVEN principles I recommend all cottages to be built; [o] on them I have formed the following plans, which I divide into four claffes or degrees. *Firft*, cottages with ONE room; *Secondly*, cottages with TWO rooms; *Thirdly*, cottages with THREE rooms; and *Fourthly*, cottages with FOUR rooms, of each of which in order.

But before I proceed, it will be proper to inform the reader, that the following plans are calculated for the neighbourhood to the *eaftward* of Bath; I fay to the *eaftward*, becaufe a little way either to the eaft, or to the weft, makes a fenfible difference in the expence of the carriage of ftone.

It is very remarkable, that if a line be drawn from north to fouth through the city of Bath, leaving the hot fprings to the eaftward, that all the ftone immediately to the eaftward [p] of that line is a fine freeftone, and continues fuch for about four miles to the eaft, when it changes to a fhelly tile, which runs about fix miles further eaftward, and then becomes a chalk in the Wiltfhire hills. Immediately on the weft of the above defcribed line, the ftone is hard, called the blue and white lyas; both will burn into lime, but the blue is the beft. This lime is very ftrong, of a brown colour, (or what the workmen term

[n] This will hold good in the country where ground is not of fo great a value, but in towns we muft be content with a fmall outlet behind. The advantage of a garden to cottages has been much infifted upon by all late writers on this fubject.

[o] I cannot more properly than in this place obferve, that near Dorchefter, in Dorfetfhire, there has been lately erected a row of four cottages for the accommodation of an adjoining Farm, in which there has not been the leaft attention paid either to the principles of found building, or to decency, or conveniency. The entrances are from the weft, and not fkreened; the windows are to the fame point; the cottages is *feventeen feet and an half* wide in the clear; and the whole triangular fpace of the roof occupied as a chamber. The confequence is, that the walls, which have not been built more than *three* years, are already confiderably fpread, and muft in a fhort time fall down; the poor inhabitants told me that they could fcarcely fupport the heat of thefe rooms in the fummer, and that they were quite frozen in the winter. The indecency of one chamber for a large Family, is here very ftriking; and what adds to the fhamelefnefs of it, was the partitions between houfe and houfe being nothing more than thin, rough boards not jointed; and yet the rent, paid for each cottage, is *fifty two fhillings* a year. It is a pity that gentlemen, who build cottages for the accommodation of their labourers, do not ftudy ftability for their own fakes, and conveniency and decency for the fake of the inhabitants: for, believe me, the poor man wifhes for conveniency, but knows not how to remedy himfelf; and would be decent, was it in his power.

[p] If this line be continued northward forty miles, even to Gloucefter, the fame circumftance of having freeftone to the eaft will ftill attend it; and if continued fouthward about twenty miles, through Shepton-Mallet, 'twill be the fame alfo, except about two miles over Mendip, where the hard lime-ftone rock runs a few miles to the eaft to Vobfter, in the parifh of Mells, and is there loft.

it, *cafts* brown) and fets or grows hard [q] under water. This lyas ftone continues for eight miles weftward, and then changes into a gritty, thin-bedded, hard ftone, called pennant, with which the foot pavements of the ftreets [r] are laid; this pennant ftone runs four miles further weftward to the city of Briftol, and then becomes a very hard lime-ftone, which cafts white, but will not fet in water. Thus at Bath we have ftone for tile; a freeftone, perhaps the fineft in the kingdom; two kinds of lime-ftone; and an excellent ftone for paving, all within an eafy carriage of the city.

The freeftone is fawed out with a common hand-faw into what is called *perpen-afhlar*, [s] that is, ftone of four, fix, eight or ten inches thick, and of fuch height and length as the rock will admit of; but generally into, what is called, ten, twelve, or fourteen inch courfes, and the ftone from two feet and an half, to four feet and an half in length. A wall well built with fix inch afhlar is much ftronger than a brick wall of nine inches thick; but if fuch fix inch walls be the external ones of any dwelling, the rooms within, as I obferved before, will be fultry hot in the fummer, and freezing cold in the winter; however, fuch thin afhlar makes moft excellent infide partitions.

Now as there is fo great a difference in the building materials, within fo fhort a fpace as ten miles either to the eaft or to the weft of one town, how much muft the materials of one country vary from thofe of another? We may therefore juftly conclude that the prices of building muft vary in every country; and yet I have found by experience, that the difference on *the whole* is very little, throughout the kingdom, if the builder is content to make ufe of the *local* materials of the country where he builds.

It has been obferved, that the eftimates for thefe cottages were made for the neighbourhood of Bath; I fhall therefore now proceed to defcribe the method of building, and the materials made ufe of in that part of the country; and alfo to fhew the prices there given not only for materials, but for workmanfhip, both by the yard, and by the day: from which premifes, I fhall lay down fuch a mode of calculation, as will put it in the power of any perfon, with very little trouble, to afcertain the value of the fame kind of work in any other country. As there are feveral branches of the building bufinefs employed in the erection of an humble cottage, I will confider and explain each feparately.

---

[q] This lime with coal afhes, mix'd in the manner prefcribed by Mr. Loriot, will make the hardeft cement I ever faw, as I have found by various experiments; it will hold water, refift froft, harden in a few hours in water, and will bear a very good polifh.

[r] The coach or carriage ways are laid, or pitched with blue lyas, which wears very well, though it will not bear the froft.

[s] A provincial term; a corruption I imagine of perpendicular, as the ftone in this form is placed on the edge, and muft of courfe be fet very plumb, or perpendicular; and the edge or bed truly fquare with the upright furface.

Masons' Work.

The materials made ufe of in this branch are *rough walling ftone* and *afhlar*. The foundation fhall be *two feet* thick, and *two feet* high to the level of the floor of the room; the walls above that level to be *twenty* inches thick; the walls of the fheds to be built with *four inch* [t] afhlar; the quoins, the jaumbs and heads of the chimneys, doors and windows [u] to be of afhlar; as alfo the fills of the windows, the fummer-ftones [w] the tabling; the tuns, or that part of the chimney that rifes above the roof, fhould be of the fame material.

A waggon load of ftones, which at the quarry cofts *one fhilling and four-pence*, and the carriage of which will be *five fhillings*, is fufficient to build a *perch* of walling confifting of *thirty* cubical feet.

Two rough mafons, [x] each of whofe wages are *three fhillings and fix-pence* for the day, and one mafon's labourer at the daily wages of *two fhillings and four-pence*, will build about *four* perch in a day, including the mixing of the mortar; thus the coft of *one* perch is *two fhillings and four-pence*, but an allowance of *one penny* is to be made in every perch for the trouble of erecting and taking down the fcaffolds, which will make the value of a perch *two fhillings and five-pence*.

Twelve bufhels of lime at *fix-pence* the bufhel; and *one* cart load of mortar dirt, or fand, at *eighteen-pence* the load (the whole making *feven fhillings and fix-pence)* will be fufficient for *three perch and an half* of work, *that is, two fhillings and two-pence* the perch.

Four inch afhlar delivered on the fpot is worth *three-pence three farthings*, and the workmanfhip in fetting the fame, and afterwards cleanfing it down, is *one penny halfpenny* for every foot fuperficial, to be meafured on one fide only; the mortar with which fuch afhlar is fet, is lime and the fand of the freeftone, but the quantity is fo fmall, that the value of what is ufed in fetting an *hundred feet* of

---

[t] In countries where there is no fuch afhlar, thofe walls muft be built as thin as poffible with the ftone of the country. And where bricks are made ufe of, a wall of the thicknefs of half a brick will anfwer the purpofe very well.

[u] This will not increafe the expence; becaufe the labour faved in hewing the quoins, jaumbs, &c. in the rough ftones, will amply pay for the extraordinary expence of the freeftone, made ufe of in thofe feveral articles.

[w] In the firft mifcellaneous plate, *Fig.* 2. A, is the *fummer ftone*; B, B, the *barge ftones*; C, the *tabling*, the firft piece of which is worked in the folid of the fummer ftone, and fo becomes an abutment, as at D, and fupport to the reft of the tabling. The tabling is *three* inches thick, and *nine* inches broad; *two* inches project over the gable end, and as the barge ftones are *four* inches thick, there are *three* inches of it to project over the covering, which makes the neateft finifh that can be imagined. The inclined plane of the gable end is called the *barge*. In walls where barge ftones are not made ufe of, their place is fupplied with a rafter, called the *barge rafter*; and this fupports the outward courfe of tile, called the *barge courfe*.

[x] The mafon that fets the ftone is called a *rough mafon*; the man that works the freeftone is called a *free mafon*; a mafon's labourer has always greater wages than a common labourer, as it requires fkill and practice to attend mafons.

four inch afhlar, will fcarcely amount to *nine-pence.*

The price, therefore, of a perch of walling will ftand thus,

	s.	d.
One load of ftone at the quarry . . .	1	4
Carriage of one load	5	0
Expence of mortar	2	2
Workmanfhip	2	5
	10	11

Now as the fame quantity of materials will do the fame quantity of work in every country where ftone is made ufe of, the above example will eafily afcertain the value of a perch of wall in any place whatfoever, in proportion to the price of materials, and in proportion to the wages of the mafon and labourer. In thofe counties where chalk and flint, or flint alone is made ufe of, the cafe will be very near the fame. And there will not be a very great difference even where they build mud-walls. I have feen thofe kind of walls, particularly in Cornwall, very ftrong and good; but if the builders would, as they lay on wet dirt, ftraw, and fmall ftones, throw in a fmall quantity of quick lime finely pounded, it would greatly ftrengthen the work; and I advife them not to be fparing of bond-timber, if they defire their buildings to be durable.

BRICKLAYERS' WORK.

This work is performed by the *rod,* containing *two hundred and feventy-two feet* fuperficial of wall *a brick and an half* thick, to which ftandard thicknefs all the walls are to be reduced. *Four thoufand and five hundred bricks* will do a rod of work; the mortar for that quantity of work will be *thirty* bufhels of lime, and two *cart* loads of fand; the mixing of the mortar will employ a labourer *three quarters* of a day; and a bricklayer and his labourer will build a rod in *five* days.

The price therefore of a rod of brick work in *London* and its neighbourhood will be as follows.

	l.	s.	d.
4500 of bricks at 42 s. the thoufand, delivered on the fpot . . .	9	9	0
30 bufhels of lime at 6 d. the bufhel, delivered on the fpot . . .	0	15	0
2 cart loads of fand at 3 s. the load, delivered on the fpot . . .	0	6	0
¾ day a labourer mixing the mortar at 3 s.	0	2	3
5 days a bricklayer at 4 s. 6 d. . .	1	2	6
5 days a labourer at 3 s.	0	15	0
	12	9	9

In countries diftant from London, where labour and materials are cheaper, the price will of courfe be lefs; for inftance, at *Stockport,* in Chefhire, the price of a rod of brick work will be as follows.

The above price of *ten fhillings and eleven pence* for the perch is the coft that every mafter-builder will be at, out of his own pocket, exclufive of his own time, of the wear and tear of fcaffolding, intereft of money, and a reafonable profit.

	l.	s.	d.
4500 bricks at 35 s. the thoufand .	7	17	6
30 bufhels of lime at 6 d. the bufhel .	0	15	0
2 cart loads of fand at 1 s. the load .	0	2	0
¾ day a man to mix the mortar at 2 s.	0	1	6
5 days a bricklayer at 3 s. the day .	0	15	0
5 days a labourer at 2 s.	0	10	0
	10	1	0

It muft here again be obferved, that thefe prices are exclufive of materials for fcaffolding, and alfo of the reafonable profit that fhould be allowed to a mafter bricklayer.

IRONMONGERY.

I mention this article before the carpenters work, becaufe there are many articles of the ironmongery goods made ufe of in the carpenters branch, and eftimated with it; the following are the chief; *four, fix, eight, ten, twelve,* and *twenty-penny* nails; *fix* inch fpikes at *two-pence* a piece; *eight, ten,* and *twelve-penny flooring brads; three, four,* and *fix-penny clout* nails; fix inch H-L *hinges,* at *one fhilling* and *two-pence* the pair; ten inch fide *hinges* at *two fhillings* and *two-pence* a pair; cafement *ftays* at *fix-pence* the pair; cafement *faftenings* at *four-pence* the pair; ftock locks at *two fhillings* apiece, and cafement fquares at *one fhilling* the fet.

CARPENTERS' WORK.

The wages of a carpenter are *four fhillings* a day, the price of fir timber *three fhillings,* and of elm *two fhillings* and *fix-pence* the foot cubical; fir board, *one inch* thick, *two pounds,* and elm board of the fame thicknefs, *one pound twelve fhillings* the hundred feet; that is, the former *five-pence,* the latter *four-pence* the foot. I muft obferve, that although fir is dearer than elm by the foot, yet it is cheaper to ufe the former, as there is fo much wafte, occafioned by the elm being in general what the workmen call very *waney.* Sawing is done by the hundred feet, from *three fhillings* and *fix-pence* to *four fhillings* the hundred; deal quarter *four* inches by *three* is worth *three-pence* the foot running.

The roofs of cottages I advife to be framed with rafters *two inches* thick; *fix inches* broad at the foot, B, *(in fig. 1. firft mifcell. Plate)* and *five inches* broad at the point, C; *tied* together by the collar piece, A, *five inches* broad, and *two* thick; *dove-tailed* at each end, as at D, D, into the rafters; *halved* together at the point, C, there faftened with *two* tenpenny nails; and *abutted* with a *bird's mouth,* as at E, E, on the wall plate, into which they are to be nailed, at the foot, with a *double tenpenny* tail; the wall plate to be *five inches* broad and *two* thick. In order to keep the roof fteady, put a ridge piece of inch board *fix inches* broad, notched on the upper edge, about *two inches* deep, to receive and clip the rafters at the internal angle of the point, and let it be drove up to its place by a collar of inch board, *fix inches* broad, which faften to the rafters with four *tenpenny* nails, as exprefled by *Fig.* 3 in the fame plate, where A is the ridge piece, and B, B, the fmall collar; *Fig.* 4, reprefents the fame ridge piece, lengthways, with the notches as above defcribed.

The pitch of the roof to be as in *Fig.* 5, in the fame plate, fuppofe a triangle A B C to reprefent the roof, where A C is the horizontal length of the bafe, or diftance from one foot of the rafter to the other, bifect the line A C at D; on the point D erect the perpendicular D E; divide A D, or C D, into four equal parts, then take three of thefe parts and fet them off on the line D E to the point B; then will A B, or C B, be the length of the rafter, and be equal to five of fuch parts as A D is divided into, by the *forty-feventh* propofition of the firft book of Euclid. For A D, the bafe, being *four*, its fquare will be *fixteen*; and D B, the perpendicular, being *three*, its fquare, will be *nine*; nine and *fixteen* make *twenty-five*, the fquare root of which is *five*, equal to the length of the rafter, or hypothenufe A B. If workmen would well confider this pitch, it would fave a deal of timber, time, and wafte. And I can affure them, from long experience, that it is fufficiently fteep for any materials that are made ufe of in this kingdom for covering of buildings.

Having mentioned above, that the rafters of the roof muft be abutted on the wall plate with a *bird's-mouth*, as at E E, referring to the firft Figure in the firft mifcellaneous plate, and as the fcale to which that figure is drawn is but fmall, and probably what I call a *bird's-mouth* may not be fufficiently underftood, it is expreffed in a larger fcale by the fixth figure in the fame plate, where A is the wall plate; B the rafter; and c d e the *bird's-mouth*. I muft obferve alfo, that the collar piece is directed to be *dove-tailed* at each end into the rafters; it muft be further directed to be kept in its place by *four* hold-fafts or ftay-hooks, fuch as are ufed by plumbers, of about the value of a *penny* each, driven through the rafters, and clinched, at the places marked with the black dots on the rafters in *the firft figure*; thefe will keep the collar piece in its place, and prevent its ftarting, without deftroying the operation of the *dove-tail*, which would certainly be the cafe if the ends of the collar piece were to be nailed to the rafters.

Wherever the roof is hip'd there muft be an angular brace of quarter, dove-tailed into the wall plate, as at A A, *Fig.* 7; the mortice to be *one inch* deep, and the under-fhoulder *half an inch*, fo that the upper fide will be *one inch and an half* above the wall plate; then let the diagonal piece C B, *fix inches* broad and *one and an half* thick, be dove-tailed, at the end B, into the brace A A, its whole thicknefs deep, then will the upper fide be flufh with the upper fide of the brace, and its under fide at C, be flat on the wall plate. This diagonal piece is the abutment to the hip rafter.

A fquare of fuch roof, including the wall plate, will contain *thirteen feet* of timber; *one hundred* feet of fawing; and *eight* feet of inch board; it will alfo require *forty* tenpenny, and *twelve* twenty penny nails; and two men will frame and put up two fquares in a day and an half. The price therefore of a fquare of fuch roofing will ftand thus,

	l.	s.	d.
13 feet of timber at 3 s.	1	19	0
8 feet of board at 5 d.	0	3	4
100 feet of fawing	0	3	6
Nails, &c.	0	1	6
Labour	0	6	0
	2	13	4

The flooring I advife to be thus, the joifts to be *fix inches* by *four*, and to lie from wall to wall the breadth of the building; two half joifts to be placed againft each end, and the remaining fpace fo divided, as to be about *three feet* from middle to middle of the joifts, as defcribed by *Fig.* 8, *in the firft mifcellaneous plate*, where A A are the half joifts, B B the whole joifts, and C C the trimmers on each fide of the chimney; then the flooring boards to be *one inch and a quarter* thick, grooved and tongued, [z] and planed on both fides. The joifts alfo fhould be planed and tried up; thefe joifts will be worth *fix-pence* the foot for the ftuff; and the planing, trying up, and laying, *two-pence* the foot running; a fquare will require *thirty-three* fuch feet; again, a man can plane, groove, tongue, and lay about *half* a fquare of flooring in a day, which amounts to *eight fhillings* the fquare; board, *one inch and a quarter* thick, is worth *fix-*

pence the foot, and a fquare of flooring will require *one hundred* of *tenpenny* flooring brads; under the ends of the joifts I would have a plate D of *inch and quarter* board, fix inches broad, laid into the wall, this will add about *eight* feet of board to every fquare. I advife alfo, that a plate of the fame fcantling, planed on the under fide only, be laid on the joifts and nailed down to them; and a fimilar plate laid along each end of the room at the fame level, the one for the fides of the flooring boards to joint to; the other to receive the heading joints, this will increafe the price of the fquare about *four fhillings*. The price therefore of a fquare will ftand thus,

	l.	s.	d.
33 feet of joifts, work included, 6 d.	0	16	6
100 feet of flooring board at 7 d. } work included	2	18	4
8 feet of plate at 7 d.	0	4	8
The extraordinary expence of the } plate above mentioned . .	0	4	0
100 tenpenny brads	0	0	10
	4	4	4

There is another method of making the naked floor, which is, to put a beam acrofs the room of *eight* inches fquare, and then the joifts to be of quarter, *four* inches by *three*, placed in the manner above defcribed; in this cafe, if the bearing of the joifts be but *five*

---

[z] *Grooved and tongued.* That is, on both edges of the board, exactly in the middle, is made a groove about three quarters of an inch deep, then a thin piece of wood, of an inch and a half broad, is put into the groove of one board, and the other is drove up to a clofe joint on it; Figure 9 in the firft mifcellaneous plate, reprefents the fection of two boards, the grooves A A on their edges, and the thin piece of board B called the tongue, all feparate; and Figure 10 reprefents the fame when clofed.

feet *eight* inches, the expence will exceed the above method a mere trifle; but if the bearing be greater, the fcantling of the joifts muft be increafed, or the joifts placed nearer together, whereby the expence will be confiderably enhanced. The former method of flooring I have found by experience to be the beft ever yet put in practice for fmall houfes, where the bearing of the joifts does not exceed twelve feet; it is attended with thefe peculiar advantages, there is no harbour for vermin; the joints of the flooring boards are fo fecured, that neither wet, nor duft, can fall from the upper to the lower floor; nor is there any occafion for lath and plaifter.

The partitions to be of boards *one inch and a quarter* thick, grooved and tongued, and planed on both fides, in the fame manner as the floors, fo the price will be *three pounds five fhillings* the fquare; that is, *three pounds two fhillings* for board and work, and *three fhillings* for nails and battens; this is to be underftood of fuch partitions as have no doors in them, for where there are doors, *two fhillings* and *fix-pence* muft be allowed for each, to pay for extraordinary labour and time, that muft neceffarily be employed in framing and hanging them, and in making the latch and catch, or fuch other faftening as fhall be thought expedient.

All doors, not in partitions, to be battened doors, with frames of quarter; every door *three* feet wide, and *fix feet four inches* high, will take *twenty-four* feet of inch board, battens included, and *eighty* tenpenny nails;

each frame will require *twenty* feet of quarter, and a man can make a well rabbetted door, its frame, hang, and put up the fame, in a day; fo that the price of a door ftands thus,

	l.	s.	d.
24 feet of inch board at 5 d.	0	10	0
22 feet of quarter at 3 d.	0	5	6
80 tenpenny nails	0	0	8
Workmanfhip	0	4	6
A pair of fide hinges	0	1	6
	1	2	2

The windows for the lower floor are to be *three* feet wide and *four feet fix inches* high; the frames of quarter; and the cafements of *inch and quarter* board; the windows of the upper floor *three* feet fquare. One of the larger windows will take *twenty-two* feet of quarter, one foot of board, and a man can make fuch frame, cafement, put up, hang the fame, and put on all the faftenings in a day, the price of the larger windows will then be,

	l.	s.	d.
22 feet of quarter at 3 d.	0	5	6
1 foot of board at 5 d.	0	0	5
Labour	0	4	6
1 fet of cafement fquares	0	1	0
1 pair of cafement ftays	0	0	3
1 pair of fix inch H-L hinges at 1 s. 2 d.	0	1	2
1 pair of cafement faftenings . . .	0	0	2
10 feet of glazing at 9 d. the foot .	0	7	6
Painting	0	0	8
	1	1	2

The fmaller windows requiring about *five* feet lefs of quarter, and about *four* feet lefs of glafs, will be worth *fixteen fhillings* each.

The ftairs to be of inch board, and the

bearings of the fame; whether the ftairs be conftructed as in plate VII, or as in plate X, the expence will be the fame, both as to materials and as to workmanfhip; but if conftructed as in plate XVIII, the expence will be a trifle more, as I fhall explain in its proper place.

The cottages being *eight feet eight inches* high, from floor to floor, there will in every ftair cafe be required, *twelve* fteps and *thirteen* rifers, in which will be ufed *fixty-four feet* of board, *eighteen feet* of quarter, *fifty* tenpenny flooring brads, and *one hundred* of tenpenny nails; a man can work, fet up, and finifh fuch a ftair cafe in two days and a half; the price therefore of a ftair cafe, will be as follows,

	l.	s.	d.
64 feet of board at 5 d.	1	6	8
18 feet of quarter at 3 d.	0	4	6
Nails	0	1	3
Workmanfhip	0	11	3
	2	3	8

Although I cannot recommend *Timber buildings*, knowing them to be attended with many and great inconveniencies, particularly their being hot in fummer and cold in winter; their being too liable to fire, and their being continually in want of repairs; yet as fome Gentlemen may be defirous of following the practice, I will give them the beft advice I

can, and this is no way better to be done, than by fhewing the method of framing the front and end of the double cottage defcribed in plate 10 of this work. The fcantling of the timber neceffary for cottages of this fort is but fmall, the ftrength of the building depending more on the mechanical conftruction, than on the fize and quantity of the materials.

All timber buildings muft be fupported on a brick or ftone foundation of about two feet high above the natural ground, on this foundation muft be laid the fill A A, *in the firft figure of the fecond mifcellaneous plate,* which reprefents the framing of the fouth fide of the above mentioned cottages; into the fill muft be tenoned the angular pofts B B, and all the other upright ftuds; the fill muft be *fix inches* broad and *three* thick, and as it will be difficult to procure timber long enough for the fill to be of one piece, let it be fcarfed or lengthened with a dove-tailed joint[a]; the ftuds a a a, that form the jaumbs of the doors and windows, are to be *fix inches* broad and *four* thick, all the others only *two inches* thick; the braces b b b, to be alfo *fix inches* by *four*; the angular pofts, B, B, fhould be in one length from top to bottom, and *fix inches* fquare. The girder C C to be tenoned at each end, into the upright pofts with a *dove-tailed*[b] *tenon*; and fcarfed with an in-

---

[a] *A dove-tailed joint.* As expreffed by the 11th figure of the firft mifcellaneous plate, at the letter A.

[b] *A dove-tailed tenon,* fee fig. 3, mifcellaneous plate 2, where A is the girder, B the upright angular poft; at the end of the girder muft be made the dove-tail tenon a b c d, the mortice b o p c muft be cut through the poft fo much longer, than the girder is high, that when the dove-tail is in its place, there will be an hole a d p o through the poft above the girder; into this hole muft be driven, tightly, the wedge C, which will always confine the tenon in its place.

dented ᶜ joint; this girder to be *fix inches* square, and its office is to fupport the floor of the chambers; the ftuds a a a, in the lower tier, are tenoned both into the fill, and into the under fide of the girder; the other ftuds only into the fill, as cutting fo many mortices in the girder would weaken it too much; but to fupply the place of a mortice, let there, between every two ftuds, be tightly driven a piece of inch board and nailed to the under fide of the girder, as expreffed by the dotted line; the fame muft be done both on the upper and lower fides of the braces as mortices to the ftuds, that reft on thofe pieces; the office of the braces is not only to keep the framing fteady, and prevent its rocking from end to end, but alfo to admit ftuff of almoft all lengths to be made ufe of; and and here I caution the builder always to place the braces leaning towards the middle of the work, and not to be guilty of that frequent error of placing them the contrary way, as I have fhewn by the dotted lines x x in the upper tier. The wall plate D D, which in thefe buildings is more properly the architrave, to be *four inches* thick, fcarfed as the girder, and dove-tailed ᵈ its whole depth into the heads of the angular pofts; the ftuds a a a, in the fecond tier, are to be tenoned both into the

girder and into the architrave, but the others only into the girder, and fecured at top as thofe in the lower tier; the fecond figure of this plate reprefents the framing of the ends, and needs no further explanation, than that the timbers A Λ, and B B, are to be tenoned into the angular pofts with a *dove-tailed* tenon, and the timber C C, tenoned into the fame pofts with a common tenon; this piece may be placed, either higher or lower, at the difcretion of the builder, as its ufe is chiefly to give an opportunity of ufing fhort ftuff.

The roofs of thefe buildings differ from thofe of ftone or brick buildings, as their office is as much to keep the oppofite fides of the building together, as to cover the cottages, and muft therefore be framed with principal rafters, as *fig.* 8, *mifcel. plate* 2, where A is the girder, or fpan beam; B B, the principal rafters; both girder and rafters are *fix inches* by *four*; the rafters to be abutted into the girder as at C, and halved together at the point; care muft be taken that the toe of the rafter at b, be within the upright of the infide of the framing; into thefe rafters muft be framed purlines of *fix* by *two*, as at c c; and at the point, between each pair of principals, muft be a ridge piece of quarter *four inches* fquare, as at D, the upper fides of

---

ᶜ *An indented joint.* This is the ftrongeft and beft way of fcarfing I ever faw, or can think of, and is explained by the fourth and fifth figures of the fecond mifcellaneous plate. Fig. 4 reprefents the pieces of timber cut into the proper fhape, but not joined; the length a b muft be about two inches fhorter than c d; and g h as much fhorter than e f; fo that when joined, *as in fig.* 5, there will be left the fquare hole B, through this hole muft be driven a double wedge, which will force the points a and h, into the angles c and f, and the beam will thereby become full as ftrong, as if it was in one piece.

ᵈ *Dove-tailed, &c.* This is explained by fig. 6 and 7 in the fecond mifcellaneous plate, where a a a a denote the head of the poft, with a proper dove-tail mortice and fhoulder; and A, in fig. 7. is the dove-tail of the wall plates.

which must bevel with the rafter, but the under fides fquare the one to the other; thefe ridge pieces muft be fupported by a fmall collar o o; on thefe purlines and ridge piece lie and are nailed the fmall rafters of *three* inches fquare; the roofs muft be always hipped at the ends, and the wall plates tied at the corners with angular braces, as in *fig.* 7, *mifcel. plate* 1, the hip rafter ferving as a brace to keep the whole roof fteady; the girders at the ends muft be calked down[c] into the wall plate with an *hidden dove-tail.*

The floors will differ from that in *the eighth figure of the firft mifcellaneous plate*, in nothing but that the ends of the joifts muft be calked down to the girder, as the girders of the roof are calked down to the wall plate; and left the ends of the joifts fhould rife, it will be neceffary to faften them with a large ftaple drove over them into the girders; but great care muft be taken not to let the ftaple pafs through the joift into the girder, as that would entirely deftroy the operation of the dove-tail, whofe office is manifeftly to keep the fides of the building from fpreading, both by thefe joifts of the floor, and by the girders of the roof; from hence will appear the reafon of fcarfing the architrave and girder with an indented joint, becaufe that method of fcarfing refifts the pull or thruft both lengthways and breadthways, whereas a dove-

tail fcarf, as in the fill, refifts only the pull lengthways.

PLAISTERERS' WORK.

There is fo little a quantity of this work required in building these cottages that it will not be worth the while of a Gentleman to provide the materials, every country plaifterer having in general by him a fufficient quantity to perform the work at *one fhilling* and *four-pence* the yard for ceilings, including laths and nails; and *eight-pence* a yard for plaiftering on walls.

TILERS' WORK.

There is no branch in the building bufinefs, except the paviours, that admits of fo great a variety as this, but there is none of greater confequence, nor that requires a greater fkill in the workman, for which reafon, the workmanfhip is always by the great. The materials made ufe of in the neighbourhood of Bath, are either *ftone tile, cornifh flate, pantile*, or *thatch;* firft then of the *ftone tile*, one waggon load will do a perch of work, confifting of two hundred and twenty-five feet, or two fquares and a quarter; at the quarry a load will coft *twenty five fhillings*; the carriage *fix fhillings*; the workmanfhip *fifteen fhillings*, and the laths *two fhillings* and *fixpence*; pins and nails *three fhillings*; and mor-

---

[c] The method of calking with an hidden dove-tail is thus: Let fig. 7, in mifcel. plate 2, be the wall plate; on the upper fide of this make a dove-tail mortice about two inches deep, as at C, with the fhoulder a b c d; on the under fide of the girder D, fig. 9, cut the dove-tail P; let this dove-tail be driven down into the mortice C, and the operation of the whole will be readily feen.

E

tar *three shillings*, in all *two pounds fourteen shillings and sixpence* the perch, or *twenty-four shillings* the square.

Of the cornish slate, fifteen hundred will do a perch, and at the sea-port will cost *twenty shillings* the thousand; the carriage *five shillings* the thousand; the dressing and laying on *fifteen shillings* the perch; the nails, laths, and mortar, the same as the stone tile, in all, *two pounds thirteen shillings and six-pence* the perch, or *twenty-four shillings* the square.

Of the pantiles *one hundred and sixty* will do a square; to the same quantity, will be required *ten, ten feet* pantile laths, and *one hundred* and *twenty* of sixpenny nails; the tiles are worth on the spot *eight shillings* the hundred; and the laths *three shillings* the dozen; and *three shillings* for the square is the price of workmanship, so that the price of a square will be *eighteen shillings and ten-pence*.

THATCH

Is of two kinds, one with haulm, or straw that has not been thrashed, but the sheaves of wheat first combed with an iron toothed comb made for that purpose, and cleared from all short straws, from weeds and grass, and then the ears cut off with a sharp sickle; the other with straw that has been thrashed. Of the first kind, eight sheaves of haulm at *twelve shillings* the dozen; *one pound* of rope yarn at *six-pence* the pound; *one hundred* of four-penny nails; and *one hundred* of *three feet* laths at *sixteen pence* the hundred, will do a square; the workmanship of which will be

three shillings and six-pence, making in the whole *thirteen shillings and eight-pence*.

Of the second kind, a ton of straw will cover six square; and straw is worth about *forty-five shillings* the ton; so that the straw, for a square, will cost *seven shillings and six-pence*; but in every other respect the expence of covering with straw is the same as covering with haulm. The first kind of thatching has this advantage, that it will last *twenty-five* or *thirty* years, whereas the second kind will require renewing every *twelve* or *fourteen* years, and there is but *six-pence* different in the price. The weekly wages of a thatcher and his boy are *twenty shillings*.

In countries where brick is the building material, the tiles are burnt ones, commonly called plain tiles. To cover a square at a *six inch* gauge, it will require *seven hundred and sixty tiles*, at *fifty shillings* the thousand; *one* bundle of laths, at *three shillings*; *six hundred* threepenny nails, a peck of pins at *one shilling*; *two* bushels of lime at *six-pence* the bushel; and *one* bushel of sand at *three-pence* the bushel; one day's work for a bricklayer at *three shillings and six-pence*, and one day for his labourer at *three shillings*; so the price of a square will stand thus,

	l.	s.	d.
760 tiles at 5 s. the hundred . . .	1	18	0
1 bundle of laths	0	3	6
600 of nails at 3 d.	0	1	6
A peck of pins	0	1	0
2 bushels of lime	0	1	0
1 bushel of sand	0	0	3
labour	0	6	6
	2	11	9

Paviours' Work.

Although this branch will admit of so great a variety, I shall confine myself to the paving proper for cottages, the rag-tile is generally made use of, and is worth *one shilling and six-pence* the yard, materials and work included; there is a kind of plaister floor much used in countries where lime and coal ashes are in plenty, it is a very good floor, and may be made for *nine-pence* the yard; where brick is the material, *thirty-two* will pave a yard square, if laid *flat ways*, and *forty-eight* if placed on *the edge*, and will be worth *four-pence* per yard for laying, so that if bricks are *two pounds two shillings* the thousand, a yard of paving flatways, will cost about *two shillings and two-pence*; and *three shillings*, if laid edgeways. Near the sea coast they pave with a small pebble, that makes very neat work, and may be done for *one shilling* the yard; flints also make no bad pavement, and is very cheap.

A SERIES

PLANS FOR COTTAGES, &c.

CLASS THE FIRST,

CONTAINING

PLANS OF COTTAGES CONSISTING OF ONE ROOM.

PLATE I.

NUMBER 1. is the moſt ſimple cottage of any, being nothing more than a room, B, *twelve feet* ſquare, and *ſeven feet and an half high* to the under ſide of the wall plate; with a porch, A, *five feet* long by *three feet eight inches* wide. The ſituation of the bed is marked with an afteriſk; the chimney is placed in the angle; and the flew of it brought round to the back, and carried up in a gable end; the cottage fronts the eaſt, and receives its light from the ſouth.

Number 2. is the cottage, having one ſhed, A, inſtead of a porch; another ſhed, C, for a pantry; and the conveniency, D; the width of theſe ſheds is determined by the pitch or declivity of the roof of the cottage; under the eaves of which the roofs of the ſheds finiſh; and their width in this and in other plans, where the whole of the cottage is on the ground floor, is *three feet eight inches* in the clear; the entrances of theſe ſheds are level with the ground, and out of them you aſcend into the cottage by

ſteps made in the thickneſs of the wall; this cottage I ſuppoſe to front either the ſouth or the eaſt, and to receive its light from that point to which it fronts; the flew of the chimney of this as well as of the foregoing, is brought up in a gable end at the back fronts, and the roof in the front is to be hipped.

Number 3. repreſents two of theſe cottages joined together; and I ſuppoſe them to receive their light from the ſouth; the chimneys are placed back to back, from whence ariſes, as well the great conveniency of having cupboards or ſhelves on each ſide of them, as the ſaving of materials.—The pantries c. c. muſt in this caſe be placed behind.—Theſe cottages, with a piece of ground for a garden, would ſerve a ſingle perſon; or two women, or a man and his wife, with one or two children.

I am well ſatisfied that it would be œconomy to build in moſt pariſhes a row or rows of theſe ſmall cots. There are many poor perſons who very much want a dwelling at a low rent, and if the parifh would at a low rent render the induftrious labourer a warm, comfortable, and healthy habitation, it would be a means oftentimes to keep him from wanting other parochial relief. The poor pitiable widow alfo, with three or four fmall children, could fhe live rent free, would be enabled, with a little other affiftance, to breed up her family; and the impotent poor, if provided for in like manner, might live comfortably on a very fmall weekly allowance.

Of this truth the Magiftracy of the Borough of St. Ives, in Cornwall, were fo well convinced, that they have erected a building from a plan of mine, containing fixteen dwellings for their impotent poor; befides a very commodious apartment for a parifh officer to inhabit, whofe bufinefs it is to infpect the conduct of the paupers, and to fee that the whole building be kept in clean and decent order; the plan of this building I fhall give in the fourth plate, with a full defcription of the fame.

The ftone of Cornwall, with which they build, is either a kind of granite called the moor ftone; or a very hard ftone, called the iron ftone; both fo hard as with the greateft difficulty to be wrought into fhape, and therefore with it they cannot build walls lefs than two feet thick; both thefe kinds of ftone, as is the cafe with all hard ftone, give, or are wet in moift weather; and therefore makes all habitations built with them unwholefome; on this confideration I recommended lining the walls with brick, and to build all the thin

partitions with the fame materials; and though bricks were fo dear at this place, that to ufe them would increafe the expence of the building full ten per cent. yet the committee, a ftriking inftance of their humanity, adopted my recommendation, declaring " they would " build habitations for their poor, fuch as " were fit for human creatures to dwell in, " and refcue them from the miferable huts " they were at prefent obliged to put up with." The expence of this building, agreeable to contract, was five hundred and fifty pounds.

PLATE II.

In this plate the length of the cottages is increafed to *fixteen* feet, the advantage of which is apparent from infpection. In numbers 1 and 2, the eaft and weft ends are gable ends, and the chimney is placed in the eaft end of each; although in number 1, it is a matter of indifference whether it be in the eaft or weft end; this number alfo varies from the fame number in the firft plate, by having the addition of the pantry, C, and of the conveniency, D. Number 3, is two of the cottages joined together.

PLATE III.

Number 1. is the plan and elevation of four adjoining cottages; each two, has a common internal porch, A. and I fuppofe a fmall garden or outlet behind each; a row of fuch cottages is what I recommended in the defcription of the firft plate, to be built in moft

F

parifhes, particularly in the manufacturing countries, for the accommodation of the induftrious poor, at a low rent. I muft here obferve, that wherever rows of cottages are to be built, be it in town or country, care muft be taken to have proper covered drains or fewers to carry off the foil and filth; there being nothing fo offenfive, not only to the public in general, but to the inhabitants themfelves, as that too common and almoft univerfal practice of throwing all the dirt and filth into the ftreet, or highway before the doors of the houfes.

Number 2. is a row of dwellings, for the parochial impotent poor. Here A is a common internal porch to the rooms D and B. The room D is for the dwelling of a pauper, that is not fo feeble, but can take care of him or herfelf; and the dwelling B, for a pauper that is able to take care of a more impotent one, that might be lodged for that purpofe by the parifh officers in the adjoining room C. Such an apartment as this would be very proper for a widow, with one or two children of her own, who might be entrufted by the parifh with two or three orphan poor children, to breed them up, till they were of an age, proper to be bound apprentices. For thefe cottages there is no occafion for the fhed behind to ferve for pantries, fufficient for that purpofe are the fhelves on each fide the chimnies. And as for the neceffaries, they are placed at each end at E, in a fmall enclofure without a roof; nor will a garden or outlet be at all neceffary.

PLATE IV.

Figure 1. is the ground plan, and figure 2, the upper floor of the building now erected at St. Ives, for the accommodation of the impotent poor of that Borough; it is fituate at the fouth weft corner of the town, at the foot of a hill that rifes pretty quick to the fouthward, it is bounded on the weft by a houfe and garden belonging to a perfon of the town, and on the fouth and eaft with ground belonging to Mr. Stephens, of Tregenna.

When I firft took a plan of the ground, the fouth weft corner, C, the north weft D, and the north eaft F, ftood as they do at prefent; but the fouth eaft corner was at H, which made the fpot of ground very awkward; on application to Mr. Stephens, he generoufly gave fo much ground as not only to make the eaft front E F, parallel to the weft front C D, and the fouth front C E fquare with, or at right angles to both, but alfo ground fufficient to make the area to the fouth.

The building confifts of eight rooms, of twelve feet fquare on the ground floor, with the fame number of equal dimenfions on the upper floor; together with the apartment marked A, and the chamber B over it, for the habitation of a proper officer to fuperintend the paupers. G G, are two conveniencies, one for the men, and the other for the women. About fixty yards up the hill, towards the fouth, rifes a large fpring of very fine water, the property of Mr. Stephens, who will permit the parifh to convey in pipes, as much water from it, into a refervoir, or bafon, in the middle of the court, as will abundantly fupply the building. The eaft front abutting on building ground, I could not enlighten any of the rooms from that point. The four ftair cafes communicate each of them to four rooms; the level of the court, is about two feet and a half above the road that leads from St. Ives to Penzance, and the floor of the lower rooms is fixteen inches above the level of the court; the ftairs are of moor ftone, and the landing place I, I, I, I, in the upper floor, are all of the fame materials; but the floors of the upper chambers are of deal, one inch and a half thick, grooved and tongued.

CLASS THE SECOND,

CONTAINING

PLANS OF COTTAGES CONSISTING OF TWO ROOMS.

THIS clafs of cottages will admit of two different modes of diftribution, that is, both the rooms may be on the ground floor, or may be placed the one above the other; of each mode in order.

PLATE V.

Number 1. This cottage is twenty-one feet long in the clear, of which fpace the room, B, occupies twelve feet and fix inches; and the bed room, C, eight feet; the entrance is fkreened with a porch, A; and behind is the fhed, D.

Number 2. is twenty five feet long in the clear, the room, B, and the bed room, C, are each ten feet wide; the porch A being on the infide, makes a very convenient recefs E for a bed, which in this fample is thrown open to the bed room C, the moft proper fituation for a bed for fmall children; and behind is the fhed, D, for a pantry.

Number 3. This cottage is twenty-nine feet long in the clear, the rooms B, and C, are both twelve feet fquare; the internal porch, A, occafions the recefs, E, as in number 2, but in this fample the recefs is thrown into the room, B, inftead of the bed room, C, for the fleeping place of an adult; the fhed, D, is here likewife added.

Number 4. This is alfo twenty-nine feet long, but the rooms B and C, being only ten feet wide, makes the bed place, D, larger than in the preceding plans, and it muft have a window, and of confequence the fhed behind cannot extend the whole length of the building, but muſt be in two parts, as E for a pantry, and F to contain the privy and a ſtore place for the fuel; the roofs of theſe ſheds may be hipped.

PLATE VI.

Number 1. Repreſents a double cottage of this ſecond claſs; I have choſen to adjoin two of the firſt number in the laſt plate a little enlarged, in order to give room for a bed in the room, A, and to ſhew in the front how the porch, inſtead of being placed on the plinth, as in the ſample aforementioned, may ſtand on the ground, and the aſcent into the cottage to be by ſteps in the thickneſs of the wall. It is very eaſy to imagine the effect of a double cottage of either of the three other examples. But a better method of building two cottages of this claſs is as,

Number 2. Where I have made an internal porch, as a common entrance to both cottages; this porch cauſes a very convenient receſs, B, for a bed, as in numbers 2 and 3, in the laſt plate.

Theſe are all the varieties of diſpoſition that cottages conſiſting of two rooms both on the ground floor, will admit of.

PLATE VII.

Number 1. is nothing more than number 2, in the firſt plate, with the addition of an upper floor, and of the ſtairs; as the ſituation of the chimney and doors will not admit of a place for a bed in the lower room, this cottage will ſuit only an artificer, with a wife,

or a wife and ſmall child, who can afford to give a little more rent than the inhabitants of the preceding cottages, ſuch as maſons, bricklayers, thatchers, plaiſterers, and many others who earn fifteen to twenty ſhillings per week; it will alſo ſuit many artificers in ſeveral branches of the manufactories, who are obliged to do their work at home; and it will be very proper for a turnpike houſe, or for a gatekeeper to any Gentleman's park.]

Number 2. By placing the chimney as in this example, a bed may be very conveniently placed in the lower room, which will render this cottage commodious to a much larger family than could poſſibly inhabit the preceding one.

PLATE VIII.

Here are two cottages adjoining of the example of No. 2, in the laſt plate, but attended with the ſmall inconvenience of leaving the pantry, B, leſs than in the ſingle one, but this is remedied by lengthening the cottage only three feet ſix inches, ſo as to have the ſtairs on the inſide, as in

PLATE IX.

Thus by placing the ſtairs on the inſide we not only gain the advantage of having a large pantry, A, to the North, but of increaſing the entrance porch, B. On viſiting the hoſpital at Froxfield, in Wiltſhire, ſome time after the engraver had ſent me a proof of this plate, I was both ſurpriſed and pleaſed to find the apartments of that ſtructure to vary but a little from this defign, the difference was in having the rooms thirteen feet wide inftead of twelve, the external door from the court, a, C, having the partition that divides the ftairs from the room, D, inclining, as reprefented by the dotted line a, b, fo as to give room for the opening of the outward door, and by the omiffion of the pantry behind.

PLATE X.

Although the plan of the cottage in the foregoing plate is very proper for the country, where there is plenty of ground, yet in towns and villages, where that may not be the cafe, it is but increafing the length of the building eighteen inches, and it will make an internal porch, and give room for the ftairs in a different form, and though there will not be convenient room for a bed below, yet this inconvenience is greatly compenfated by the recefs, A, in the chamber above; indeed by letting the ftairs begin to rife from the porch, A, on the ground floor, there may be room for a bed below, as in the foregoing plan, but this is only admiffible in country villages, but not in large towns or cities, for reasons I fhall give in defcribing the following plates; a number of thefe cottages built in villages would be of great fervice, and though to private perfons they probably may not anfwer in regard to interest of money, yet if built at a parochial expence they would anfwer the purpofe of accommodating the induftrious labourer with a family at a fmall and eafy rent.

PLATE XI.

Here I join four cottages together, and it is an eafy matter to imagine a continuation of them to any number; thefe are proper for large towns or cities, in two of thefe plans the ftairs from the lower room, A, begin to rife at D, and will land at the chamber, C, above, which caufes the door, E, to be near the head of the bed; but in the other two the ftairs from the room, B, begin to rife at F, which land at G, in the chamber, D, above, whereby the bed will be better fcreened, but the builder may take his choice of either method. If thefe cottages are built in large towns or cities, by all means avoid letting the ftairs begin to rife from the porch fo as to make room for a bed below, in order to prevent any avaricious inhabitant taking an inmate; an inconvenience felt by moft parifhes, though I muft own there fhould be fome care taken to provide for fingle perfons wanting lodgings; but more of this in defcribing the cottages of the third and fourth clafs. In thefe dwellings, if it can be done, let there be an outlet or fmall garden to admit of the pantry, C, the wafh place, B, the conveniency, P, which will keep the whole fweet and wholefome.

G

CLASS THE THIRD,

PLANS OF COTTAGES CONSISTING OF THREE ROOMS.

THIS clafs of cottages will admit of four different modes of diftribution, 1ft. All the rooms on the ground floor;—2dly. Two rooms below, and one above;—3dly. One room below, and two above;—4thly. The three rooms one above the other. The firft mode of diftribution will admit of no lefs than eleven variations.

PLATE XII.

This plate contains two varieties of the firft mode of diftribution.

Number 1. is thirty feet long in the clear, of which the two rooms, D and G, take ten feet each, and the room, F, nine feet. The entrance to this cottage is on the north fide at the porch, A, on one fide of which is the ftore place, B, and on the other fide the pantry, E; from the porch, A, you afcend into the paffage, C, by two fteps in the thicknefs of the wall.

Number 2. is thirty-four feet fix inches long in the clear, of which the central room, B, takes twelve feet; the room, F, nine feet; the room, G, ten feet nine inches, and the remaining fpace is occupied by the wall and partition. The entrance is on the eaft by the paffage, A; the floor of the pantry, C, is level with the floor of the room, B, and this pantry may be made of any width you pleafe. The roof is hipped into the roof of the main building, as fhewn in the north front, D is the ftore place.

PLATE XIII.

This plate alfo contains two other varieties of the firft mode of diftribution. The entrance of Number 1. is from the fouth into the internal porch, A, which communicates to the rooms, B and C, each ten feet wide; from B, is the door not only into the pantry, E, but into the fleeping room, D, which projects about three feet and fix inches northwards, and its roof hipped into the roof of the main building, as fhewn in the north front. This room is fuppofed to be a bed place for an adult, and the clofet, F, is adjoining to it.

Into Number 2. you likewife enter from the fouth, A is an internal porch of a larger dimenfion than any of the preceding, and communicates to the bed room, D, and into the room, B; a, is a recefs for fhelves. The room, D, is ten feet wide, and the room, C, is of the fame dimenfion; E is the pantry, and F the ftore place, in the corner of which is intended a flew to go into the main ftack.

PLATE XIV.

Of the fame mode of diftribution here are two more varieties.

The room, B, in Number 1. is fourteen feet and a half long, and the entrance fcreened by the porch, A; in the corner is a place for a bed. The bed room, C, is ten feet wide, and the room, D, eight feet; this room is placed behind, and lighted from the north, in order to ferve for a work-fhop, as well as a bed room, there being many branches, not only of the woollen, leather, cotton, and Manchefter manufactories, as well as feveral others, in which the workmen perform their work at home, and require a ftrong and fteady north light. Should this cottage be intended for a weaver, the back room muft be extended more to the northward.

Number 2. differs from the former, in having the porch, A, on the infide; this reduces the room, B, to ten feet wide, and forms the recefs, d, for a bed, which may be either thrown to the room, C, as in this plate, or to the room, B, as in Number 3 of the fifth plate. In both plans, E is the pantry, and F the ftore place.

PALTE XV.

Number 1 and 2 of this plate cannot be fo properly called varieties, as improvements on the two examples in the laft plate, viz. by enlarging the room, D, putting a fire place in it, and altering the fituation of the chimney in the bed room, C, by placing it further from the bed. In the north front, inftead of hipping the roof of the projecting room, it is carried up as a gable end. Number 3 is but a fimilar improvement of Number 2 in the thirteenth plate, the fouth front of which is the fame with this; and the fouth front of the two in the laft plate, are the fame with the correfponding ones in this plate.

PLATE XVI.

Number 1. is two of the cottages given in Number 1, Plate 13, and joined together. I have only increafed the width of the bed place, D, and made the entrance into it from the room, C, as I fuppofe it to be the bed place of girls or of children who fhould be more immediately under the care of the mother; o, fhews where a flew may be placed to be drawn into the ftack.

Number 2. is a plan for two adjoining cottages on an entirely different conftruction from the foregoing, and I think more convenient. On this plan a regularity of Front can be preferved, which cannot be done in a fingle cottage. Here is an internal porch, A, that communicates to the chamber, D, and to the room, B, and makes the ufeful recefs, d. From B, you go into the chamber, C; the pantry, E, is conftructed as in No. 2, Plate 12, except in the recefs, g, where may be placed a flew.

PLATE XVII.

Number 1. is the only example I can give of this third clafs of cottages, according to the fecond mode of diftribution, that is, with two rooms below and one above, and it needs no further defcription, than that the entrance is at the fide at A, which leads to the room, B, adjoining to which is the chamber, D, and over B, is the chamber, E.   C is the pantry.

Number 2. This is alfo the only example of the third clafs of cottages according to the third mode of diftribution, but I am of opinion would prove the moft ufeful dwelling of any, as it admits conveniently of room for three beds. This cottage I make fixteen and a half feet long in the clear; A is the entrance porch, C the pantry, and B the dwelling room; the ftairs are fix feet ten inches by fix feet, and being placed directly in the middle of the back Front, gives fufficient room to get up to the upper or chamber floor, and by making a ftep in the thicknefs of the wall above, there will be fufficient head room for the ftairs to be covered with a fkeeling roof. The upper floor is divided into two rooms by a boarded partition. In the execution of this cottage and in the following ones of two rooms in the upper floor, and where the ftairs are placed in the outfide—and are intended to be covered with a fkeeling or fhed roof, great care muft be taken to obferve the dimenfion of fix feet ten inches by fix feet, not only to give head room for the ftairs, but to make a pier between the doors that lead from the ftairs into the chambers D. Although I here propofe to have the ftairs covered with a fhed roof, I cannot but recommend the carrying of the walls of the ftairs to the level of the walls of the cottage, and then hipping the roof into that of the cottage; in this cafe there will be no occafion for the ftep in the thicknefs of the wall, but the wall may be thinned as in No. 2. Plate 13. or as expreffed by Fig. 3. in the mifcellaneous Plate, ftill the ftairs muft be fix feet ten inches by fix feet; but you muft begin with a winder, and land above in the fame manner.

PLATE XVIII.

In this plate two of the foregoing cottages are joined together, in which cafe the pantries C C, will be on each fide of the ftairs.

PLATE XIX.

In this example of the two adjoining cottages of the third clafs, I omit the fhed at each end, and make the cottage nineteen feet long, inftead of fixteen and a half in the clear; here then will be an internal porch, A, which admits of a recefs for a bed in the lower room, which will render the upper chambers larger; c the wafh place, m the flew, d the pantry. It will be moft convenient to make that which has the fire place in it, larger than the other, for many obvious reafons, as fhewn in the plan. Care muft be taken to place the middle of the ftairs to anfwer exactly with the partition above, to give room for the doors into the chambers, and the pier between them.

PLATE XX.

An example of a fingle cottage according to the fourth mode of diftribution, would be prepofterous in the elevation, fo that I only give an example of two fuch cottages adjoining each other, fuited for the country. The plan explains itfelf, only I muft obferve that in the upper floor there are no fire places, nor are they wanted. The breaks in the party wall are to receive the flews of the chimneys below, in order to bring them regularly out above the roof.

PLATE XXI.

In cities and large towns I cannot but think that a row of fuch dwellings as are defcribed in this plate, would be of great fervice, if built at a parochial expence, to accommodate fuch of their labouring workmen who are parifhioners, and can afford to give a moderate, though not an extravagant or large rent for their habitations. The entrance is by an internal porch, A, five feet nine inches deep by fix feet wide; the ftairs, which are fix feet fquare, communicate diftinctly to both the upper chambers, in which the receffes over the porch afford good room for a child's bed.

It is very apparent that the approach to the ftairs may be from the porch, A, inftead of being from the room, B, in which cafe this building would become three diftinct habitations; a circumftance to be avoided, in order to prevent an avaricious tenant taking in inmates, and thereby defeat the end of accommodating an induftrious workman.

CLASS THE FOURTH,

CONTAINING

PLANS OF COTTAGES CONSISTING OF FOUR ROOMS.

We are now come to the largeft fize cottages; there are only two methods of placing the rooms of this clafs, and that is either, firft, all the rooms on the ground floor;—or, fecondly, two rooms below and two above.

PLATE XXII.

Number 1. is of the firft mode of diftribution. This cottage is forty-nine feet fix inches in the clear, the bed rooms, B and E,

H

eleven feet each, and the bed room, C, nine feet; the dotted lines in this room fhew where a fcreen or partition may be placed; H the paffage to the wafh place F, with the flew m, as alfo to the pantry G, in which a is a recefs for a cupboard.

Number 2. is of the fame extent in the clear as Number 1. A an internal porch, D the dwelling room; C the bed room of thirteen feet fix inches; B a bed room for children or girls, in which they will be under the care of their mother; E a bed chamber fit for an adult; F is the pantry; H the wafh place, to which you descend by two fteps in the thicknefs of the wall; o the flew, g a ftore place.

PLATE XXIII.

This cottage differs from any of the former, in having neither an external nor internal porch. It is thirty-one feet in the clear, where A may be either the dwelling room, or it may more properly be ufed as a work-fhop fuitable for fome occupations, having an immediate accefs to it from the ftreet; in the former cafe F will be the pantry, and in the latter an appendage to the fhop; B C D are bed rooms, and E a paffage; G a wafh place, with the flew o, which may be drawn into the main ftack.

PLATE XXIV.

To this cottage is intended a garden behind; it is thirty feet fix inches in the clear;

the bed rooms, B and C, are eleven feet fix inches each; the bed room, D, to the north, muft be carried up as in plate 15; I a paffage which communicates with the pantries F and H, and to the wafh place E, and the ftore place G. The dotted lines fhew where a fcreen or curtain may be placed to divide the dwelling room A, from the paffage, to render it warm.

PLATE XXV.

Each of thefe cottages are thirty-four feet in the clear; the bed room, C, ten feet; and the bed room, B, feven feet fix inches. F is the pantry, and E the wafh place. D is a large bed room, in which one or two Females may lodge, and in that cafe b will be their conveniency, and a the conveniency for the males.

PLATE XXVI.

This is the fecond mode of diftribution of the fourth clafs. In Number 1. there is no chimney in the bed room, C, but a pier or break to carry the fire place in the room above. D D is a pantry and wafh place, where a a fhew the flews. The ftaircafe is placed in the back part, as in Plate 19, and muft be carried up in the fame manner, to give room for the doors to the bed rooms as well as the pier between them. Number 2. the internal porch A, forms a recefs for the ftaircafe, alfo a leffer one for a cupboard; D the pantry, b the flew. The ftairs land above the lobby or paffage, E, which communicates to the bed rooms, L L.

PLATE XXVII.

Is the plan of two adjoining cottages, in which there are not any porches, c being ufed as the dwelling room or work fhop. This plan admits of three bed rooms; the ftairs muft be carried in the fame manner as de-

fcribed in the laft plate, Number 1. D is the pantry, and *b* a flew.

PLATE XXVIII.

Is the plan of two adjoining cottages, the fame as the example of the fingle cottages, Plate 26, Number 2, with the difference of D being the pantry, and E the wafh place.

THE END.

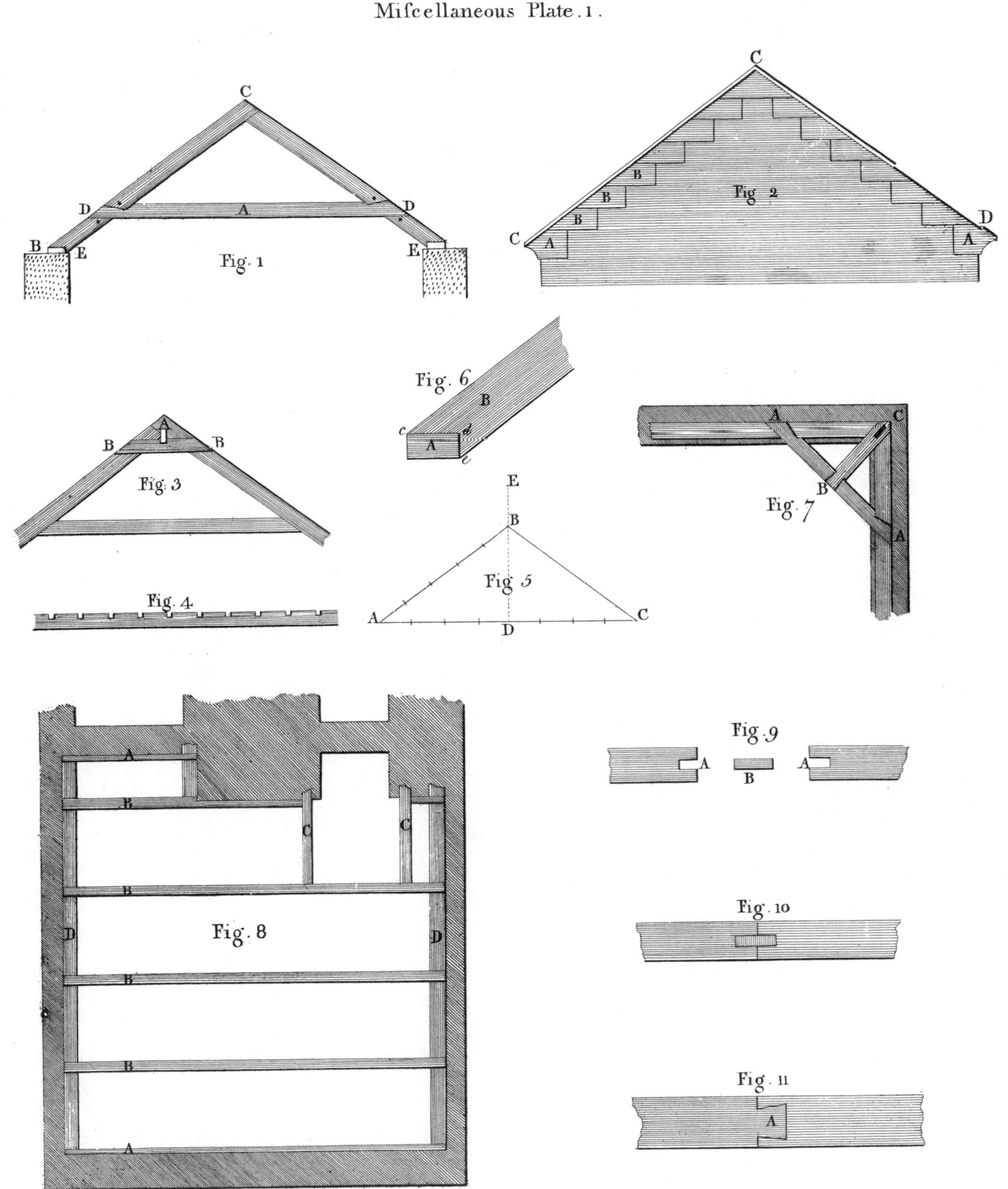

Fig. 1

Fig. 2

Fig. 3

Fig. 4

Fig. 5

Fig. 6

Fig. 7

Fig. 8

Fig. 9

Fig. 10

Fig. 11

Engraved at the expence of John Wood, Architect, after his own original designs and published by him Jan:y 1st 1781

P. Begbie Sculpt

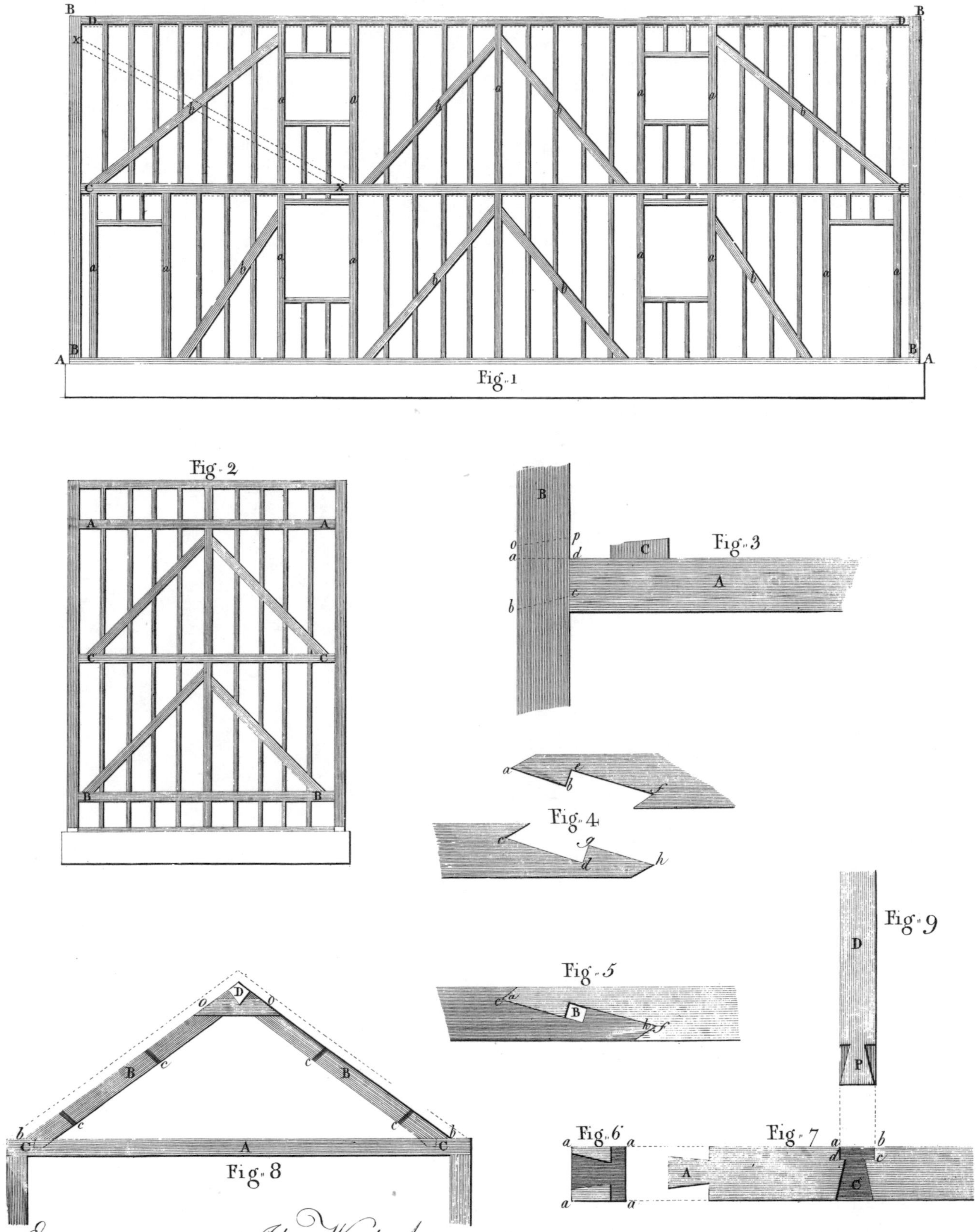

Engraved at the expence of John Wood, Architect, after his own original designs and published by him Jan.ry 1.st 1781

P. Begbie Sculp.t

Fig. 8

Fig. 7

Fig. 6

Fig. 5

Fig. 9

Fig. 4

Fig. 3

Fig. 2

Fig. 1

Miscellaneous Plate. 2.

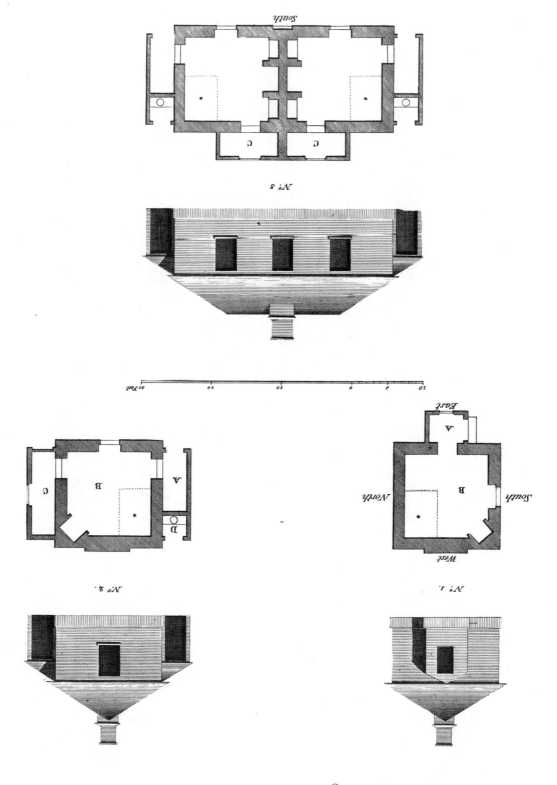

Engraved at the expense of John Wood, Architect, after his own original designs and published by him Jan.y 1.st 1781.

P. Begbie Sculp.

South

N.o 3

East

North   South

West

N.o 1.

C   B   A

D

N.o 2.

Cottages with one Room

Plate 1.

Class 1.

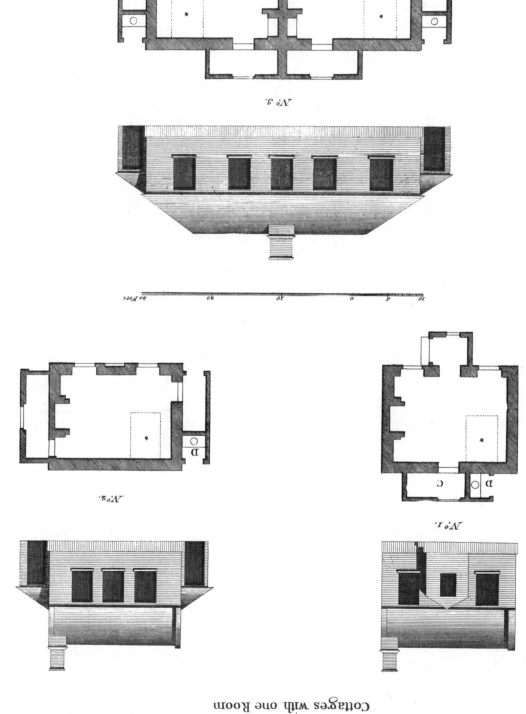

Engraved at the expence of John Wood, Architect, after his own original designs and published by him Jan.ʳ 1ˢᵗ 1781.

P.Right Sculp.ᵗ

Nº 3.

Nº 2.

Nº 1.

10 4 0 10 20 30 40 50 Feet.

Plate II.

Cottages with one Room

Class 1.

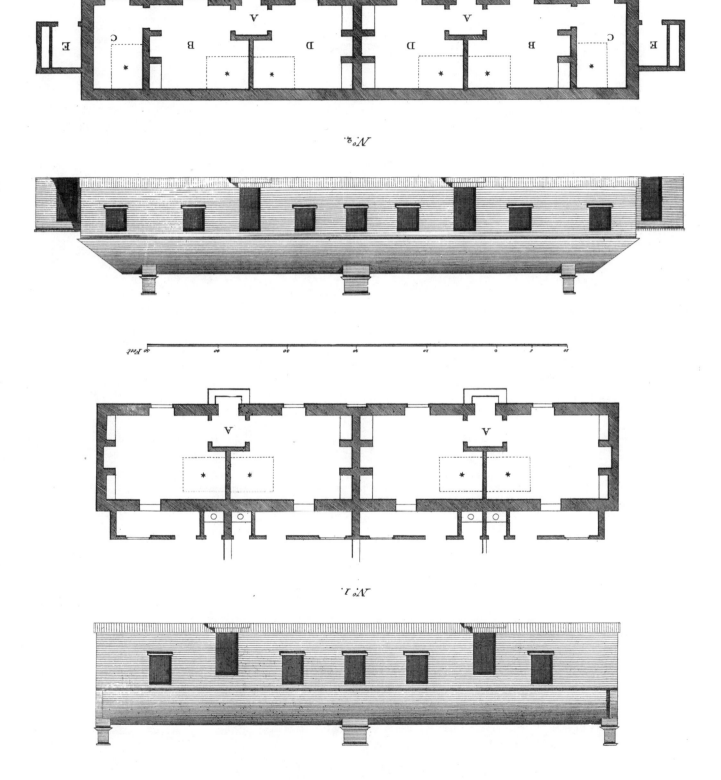

Engraved at the expense of John Wood, Architect, after his own original designs and published by him Jan.ʸ 4.ᵗʰ 1781.

P.Begbie Sculp.ᵗ

Nº 2.

Nº 1.

Plate III

Cottages with one Room

Class I.

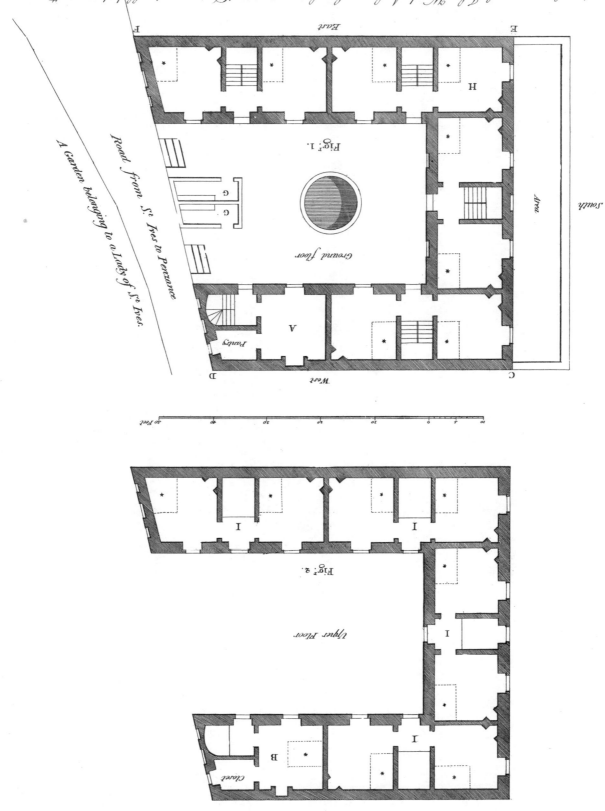

Engraved at the expence of John Wood Architect after his own original Designs, and published Jan.ʳ 1.ˢᵗ 1781.

P. Begbie sculp.ᵗ

East

South

Area

H

Fig.ᵗ 1.

Ground floor

G
G

Road from S.ᵗ Ives to Penzance

A Garten belonging to a Lady of S.ᵗ Ives.

A

Pantry

West

D   C

Fig.ᵗ 2.

I   I

Upper Floor

I

B
Closet
I

Plate IV.

Cottages with one Room

Class I.

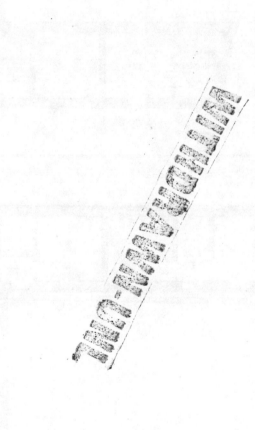

INTRODUCTION

Engraved at the expence of John Wood, Architect after his own original designs and published by him Jan.ʸ 1.ᵗ 1781.

P.Begbie Sculp.ᵗ

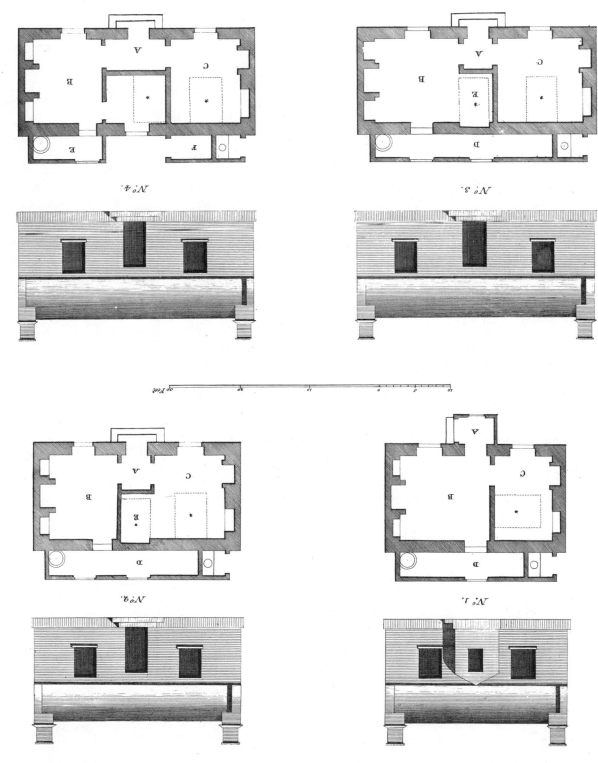

N.º 4.

N.º 3.

10 Feet 5 0 10 20 30 40 50 Feet

N.º 2.

N.º 1.

Plate V.

Cottages with two Rooms

Class 2.

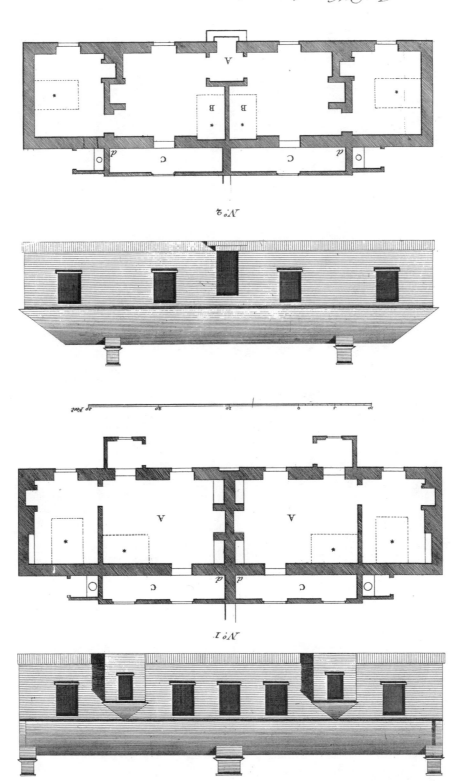

Engraved at the expence of John Wood, Architect, after his own original designs and published by him Jan.ʳ 1ˢᵗ 1781.

T. Bogen Sculp.

No. 2

No. 1

Class 2   Cottages with two Rooms.   Plate VI.

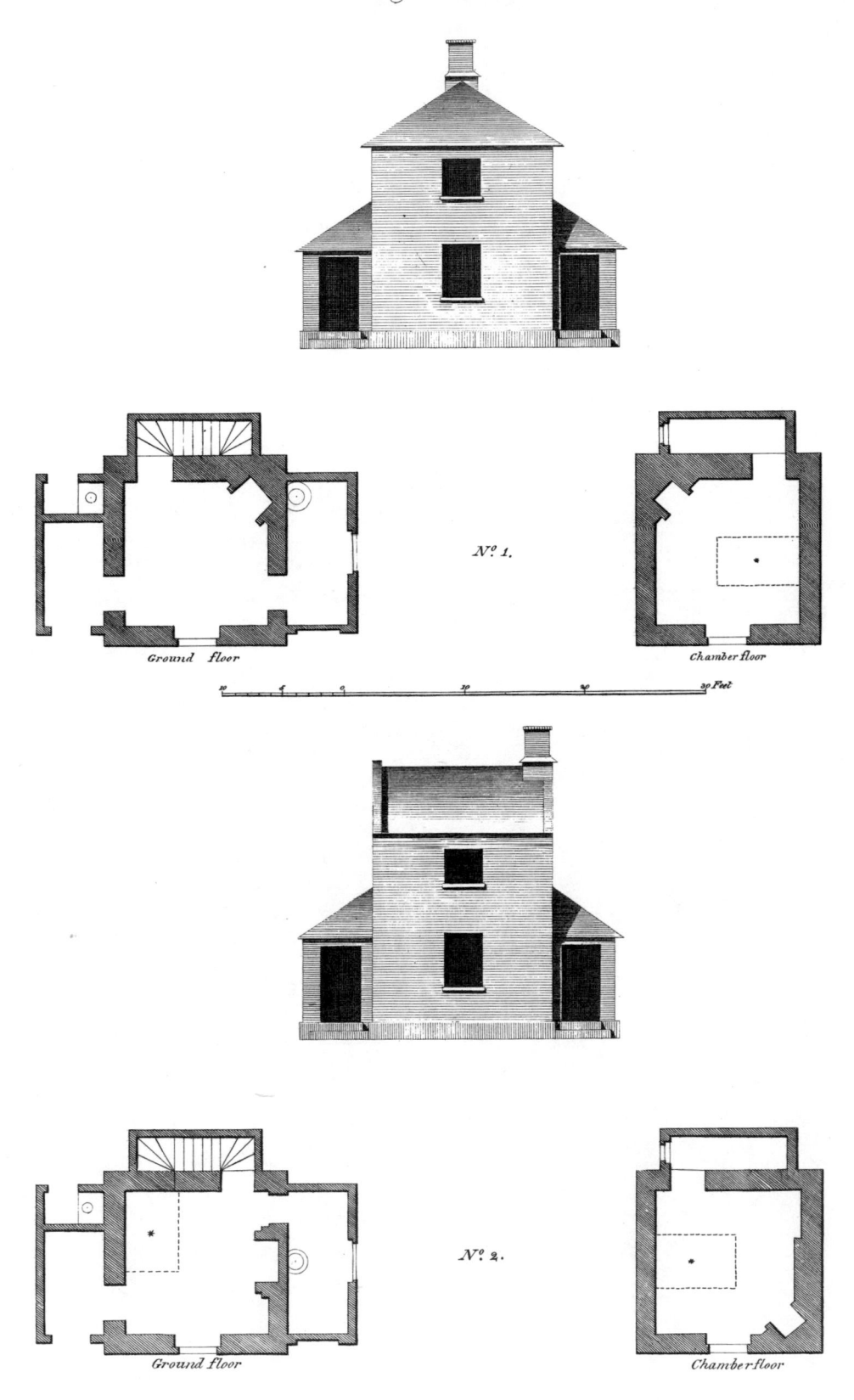

Nº 1.

Ground floor   Chamber floor

Nº 2.

Ground floor   Chamber floor

Engraved at the expence of John Wood, Architect, after his own original designs and published by him Jan.ᵈ 1ˢᵗ 1781

P. Begbie Sculp.ᵗ

Ground Floor

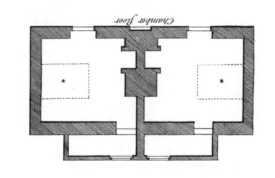

Chamber floor

30 Feet

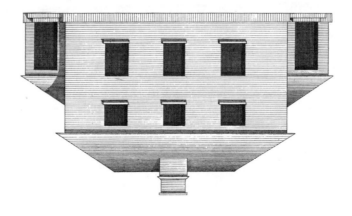

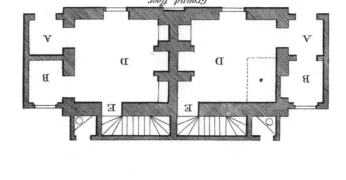

Engraved at the expense of John Wood Architect after his own original designs and published by him Jan.y 1.st 1781.
F.Begbie Sculp.t

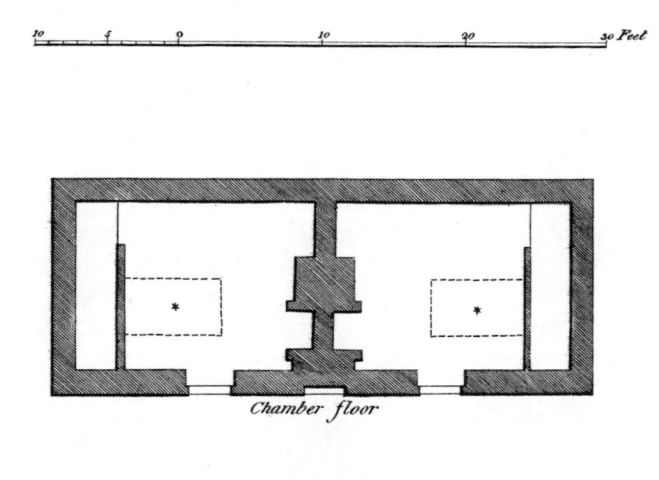

Chamber floor

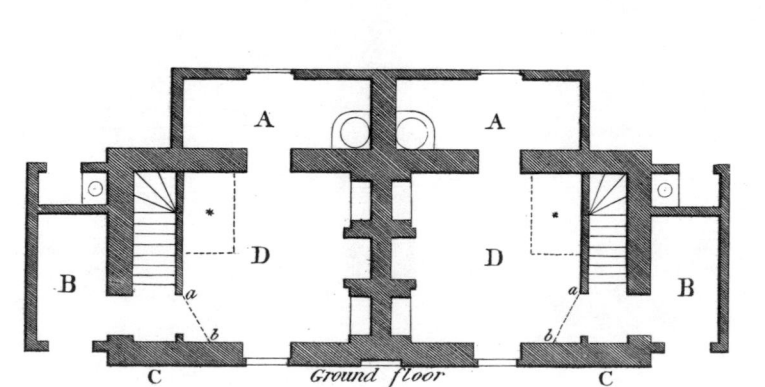

Ground floor

Engraved at the expence of *John Wood, Architect, after his own original designs and published by him* Jan.ʳᵈ 1.ˢᵗ 1781

P. Begbie Sculp.ᵗ

Engraved at the expense of John Wood, Architect, after his own original designs and published by him Jan.ʳ 1ˢᵗ 1781.

P.Begbie Sculp.ᵗ

Plate 2.

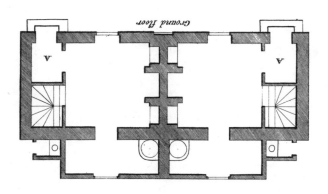

Ground Floor

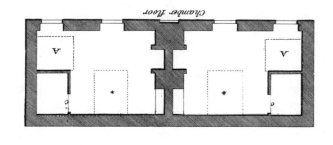

Chamber Floor

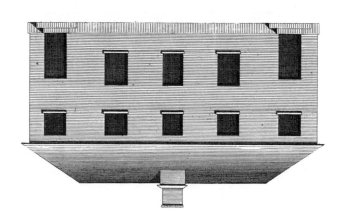

30 Feet

Plate x.

Cottages with two Rooms

Plate 2.

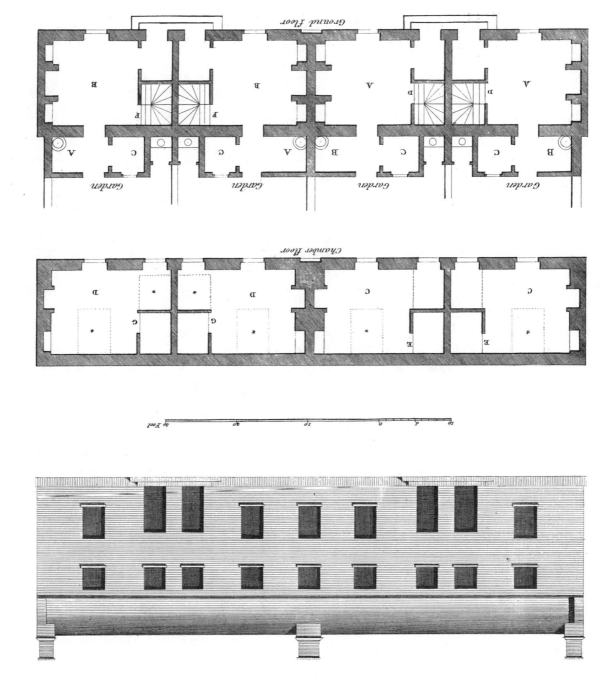

Ground Floor

Chamber Floor

Garden

Plate xi.

Cottages with Two Rooms

Claſs 2.

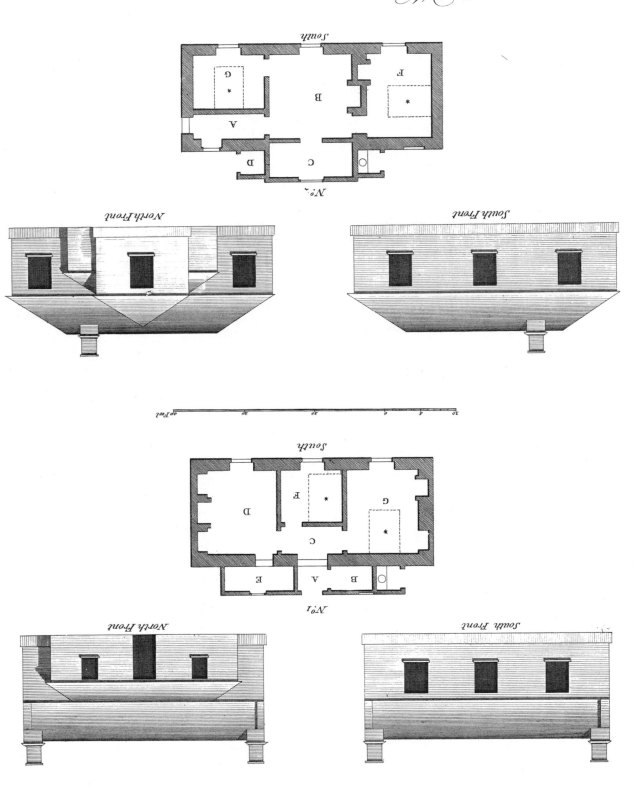

Engraved at the expense of John Wood, Architect, after his own original designs and published by him Jan.ʳ 1.ˢᵗ 1781.
I.Begbie Sculp.ᵗ

Plate XII.

Cottages with three Rooms

Class 3.

Engraved at the expense of John Wood, Architect after his own original designs and published by him. Jan.ʳ 1.ˢᵗ 1781.

P. Begbie Sculp.ᵗ

South Front

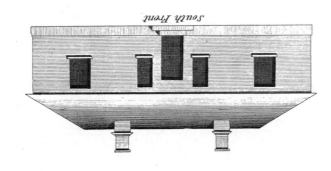

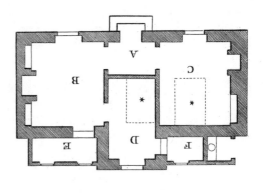

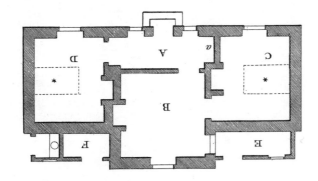

South Front

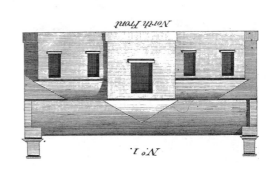

North Front

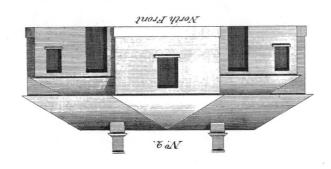

North Front

N°. 2.

N°. 1.

Plate XIII.

Cottages with three Rooms

Class 3.

Engraved at the expense of John Wood, Architect, after his own original designs and published by him. March 1st 1778.

P. Begbie Sculp.

South Front

South Front

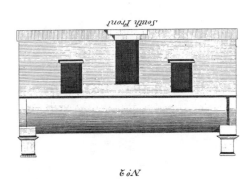

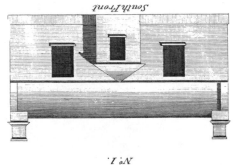

No 2.

No 1.

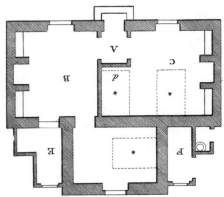

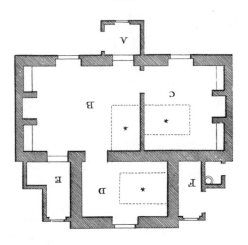

North Front both to No 1 and to No 2

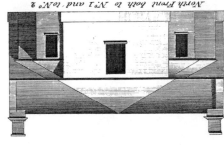

Plate xiv.

Cottages with three Rooms

Class 3.

Engraved at the expense of *John Wood*, Architect, after his own original designs and published by him. *Jan.ʳ 1.ˢᵗ 1781*

P.Begbie Sculp.ᵗ

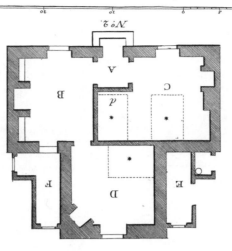

No. 2.

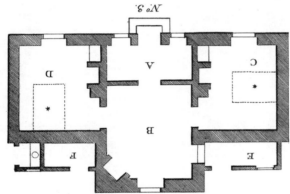

No. 3.

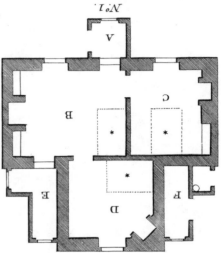

No. 1.

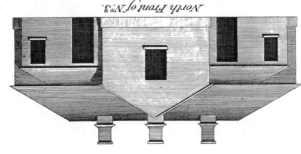

North Front of N.º 3.

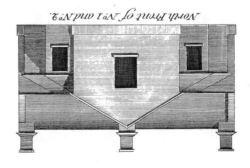

North Front of N.º 1 and N.º 2.

Plate XV.

Cottages with three Rooms

Class 3.

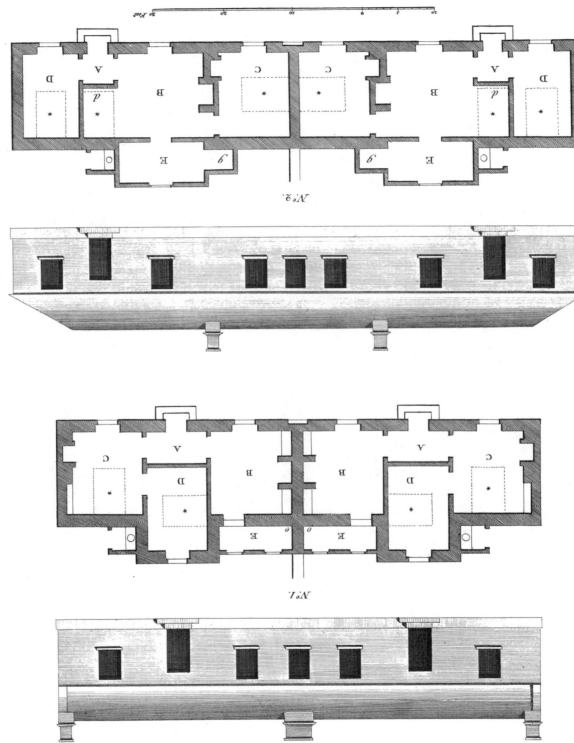

Engraved at the expense of John Wood, Architect, after his own original designs and published by him. Jan.ᵗʰ 1ˢᵗ 1781.
P.Begbie Sculp.ᵗ

N.º 2.

N.º 1.

Plate XVI.   Cottages with three Rooms   Class 3.

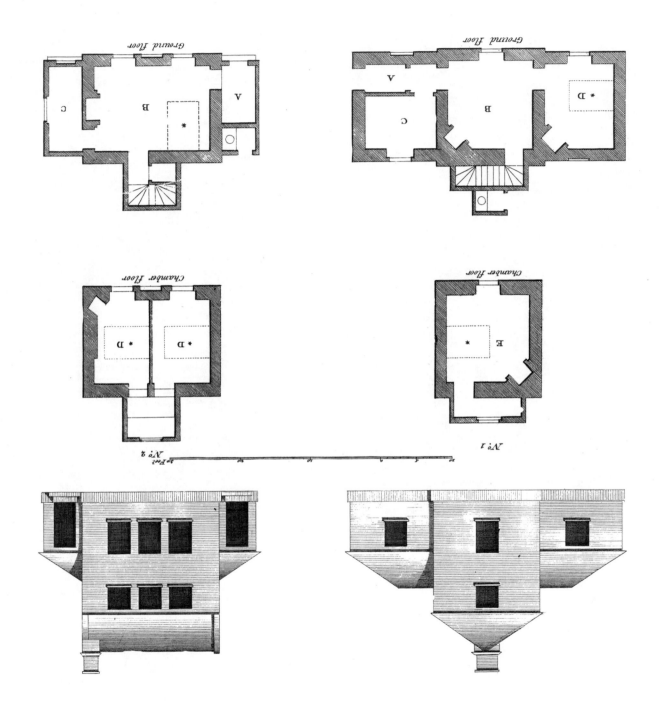

Engraved at the expense of John Wood, Architect after his own original designs and published by him Jan.y 1.st 1781

Bright Sculp.

Ground Floor

Chamber Floor

N.o 2

N.o 1

10 Feet

Plate XVII.

Cottages with three Rooms

Engraved at the expence of John Wood, Architect, after his own original designs and published by him Jan. 1. 1781.

P.Begbie Sculp.

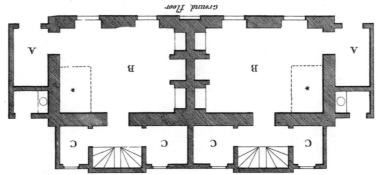

Ground Floor

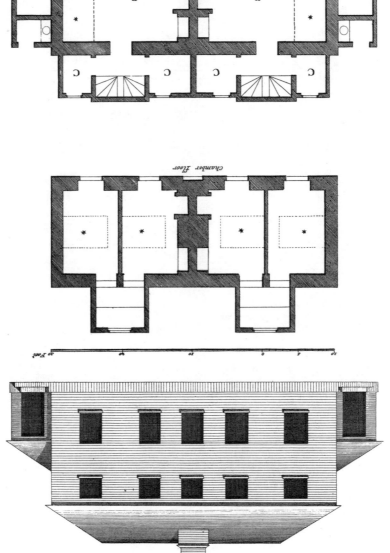

Chamber Floor

10 5 0 10 20 30 40 Feet

Engraved at the expense of John Wood, Architect after his own original designs and published by him Jan.y 1st 1781

P.Begbie Sculp.t

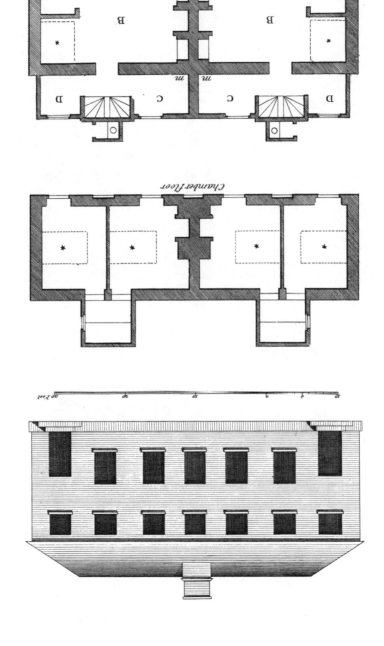

Ground Floor

Chamber Floor

Feet

Plate XIX.

Cottages with three Rooms

Engraved at the expense of John Wood, Architect, after his own original designs and published by him Jan.ʳ 1.ˢᵗ 1781.

P. Begbie Sculp.

Ground Floor

Upper Floor

2.ᵈ Floor

10   5   0   1   2   3   4   5   10   20   30   40 Feet

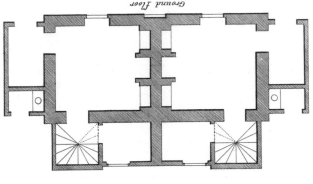
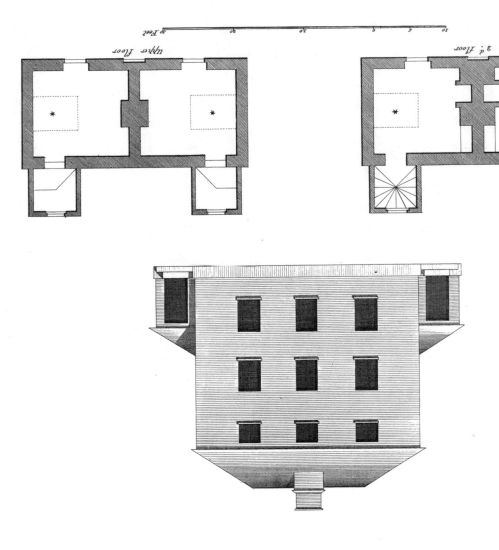

Plate XX.

Cottages with three Rooms

Engraved at the expence of John Wood, Architect, after his own original designs and published by him Jan.ʳ 1ˢᵗ 1781.

P.Begbie Sculp.

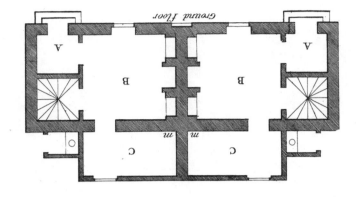

Ground Floor

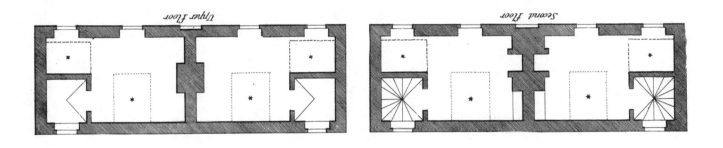

Upper Floor

Second Floor

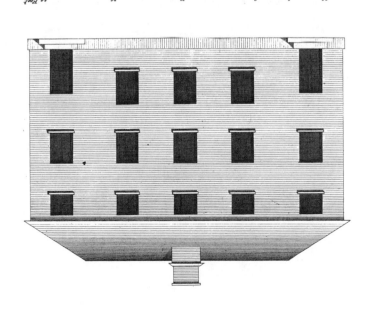

10 Feet

Plate xxi.

Cottages with three Rooms

Class 3.

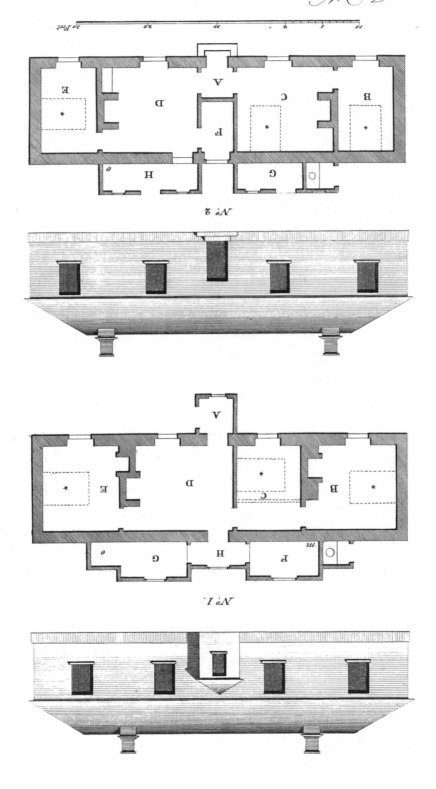

Engraved at the expence of John Wood, Architect, after his own original designs and published by him. Jan.ry 1. 1781.

P. Begbie Sculp.

No 2.

No 1.

Engraved at the expense of John Wood Architect at his own original designs and published by him Jan.ᵘ 1.ˢᵗ 1781

P.Begbie Sculp:

South Front

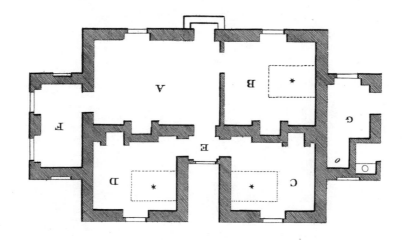

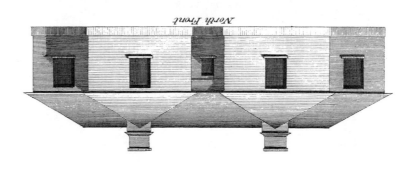

North Front

Plate xxiii

Cottages with four Rooms

Clafs 4.

Engraved at the expence of John Wood, Architect after his own original designs and published by him. Jan.y 1.st 1781

F. Begbie Sculp.

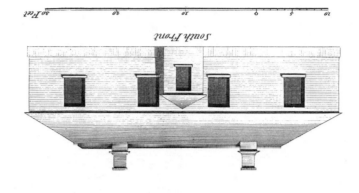

South Front

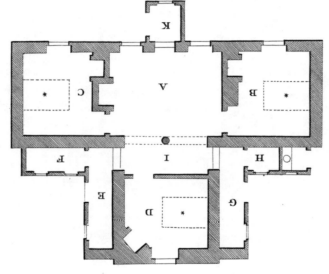

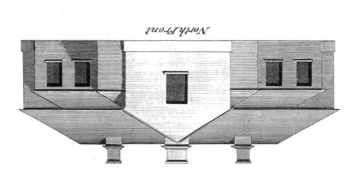

North Front

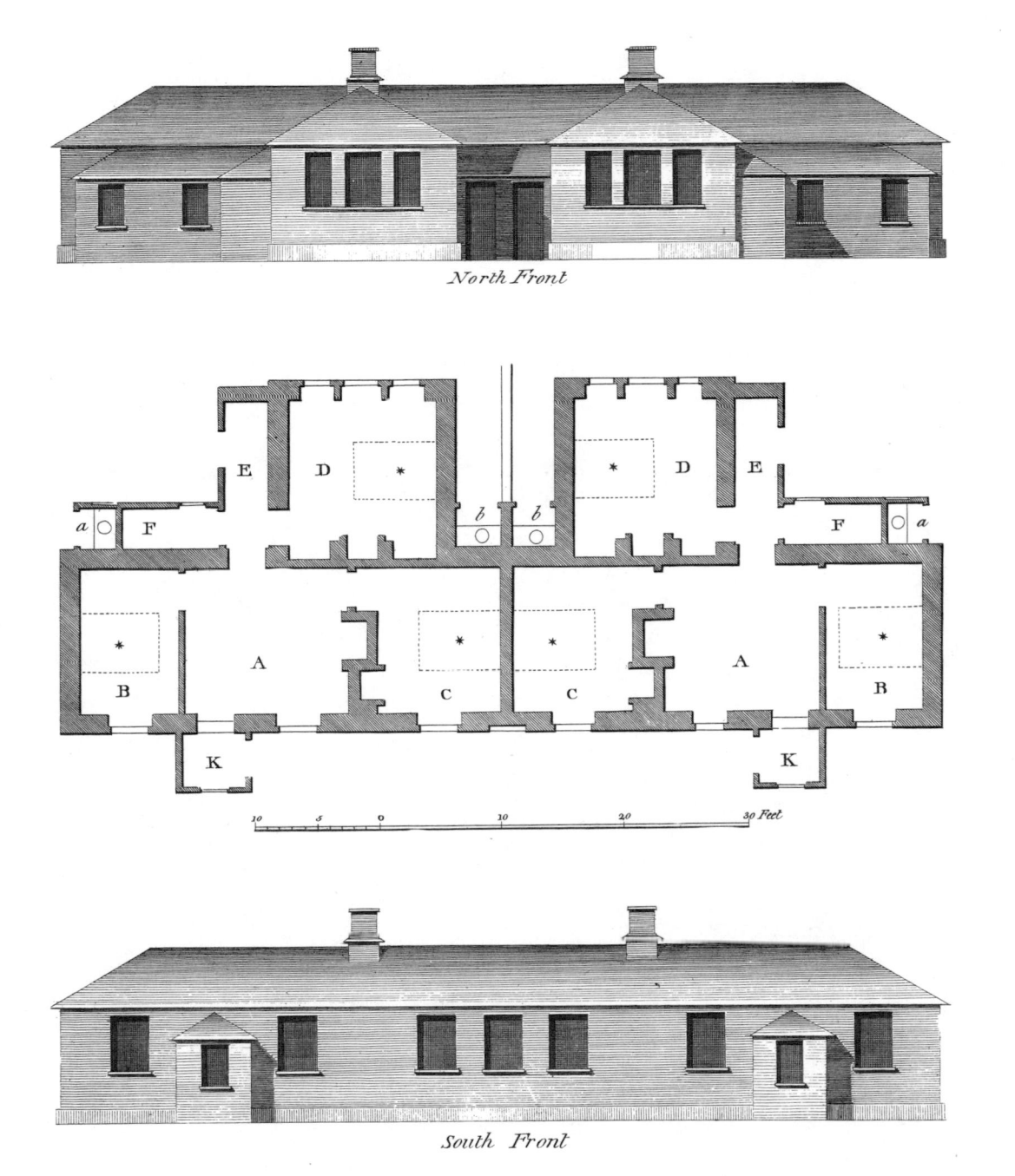

North Front

South Front

Engraved at the expence of John Wood, Architect, after his own original designs and published by him Jan.ʸ 1.ˢᵗ 1781

P. Begbie Sculp.ᵗ

No.1.

Chamber Floor

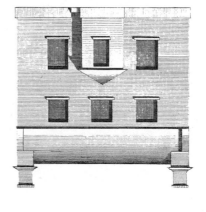

Ground Floor

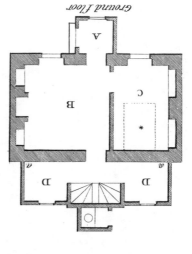

A

B

C

D

No.2.

Chamber Floor

E

I

I

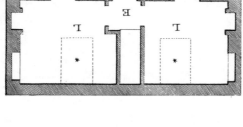
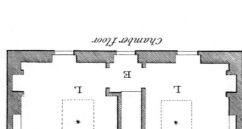

Ground Floor

A

B

C

D

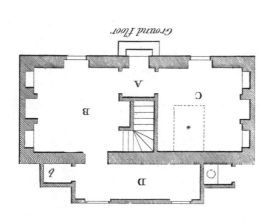

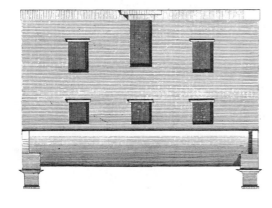

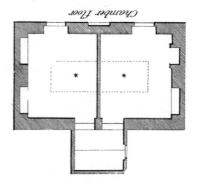

Engraved at the expence of John Wood, Architect after his own original designs and published by him Jan.ry 1, 1781.
P.Begbie Sculp.

20   10   5   0   10   20   30   40 Feet

Engraved at the expense of John Wood, Architect, after his own original designs and published by him Jan.ʳʸ 1.ˢᵗ 1781.

P. Begbie Sculp.ᵗ

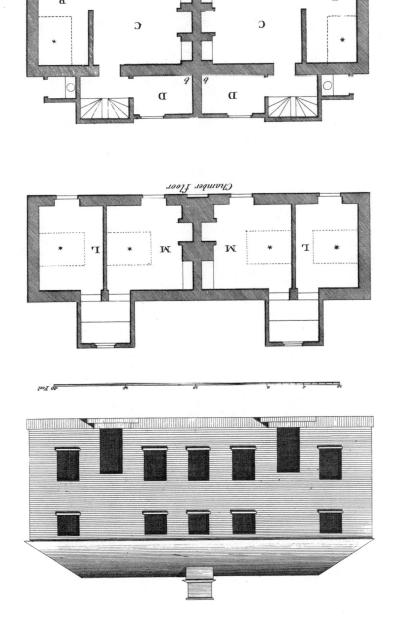

Ground Floor

Chamber Floor

40 Feet

Plate XXVII

Cottages with four Rooms

Class 4.

Engraved at the expence of John Wood, Architect after his own original designs and published by him Jan.ʳ 1.ˢᵗ 1781

P.Begbie Sculp.ᵗ

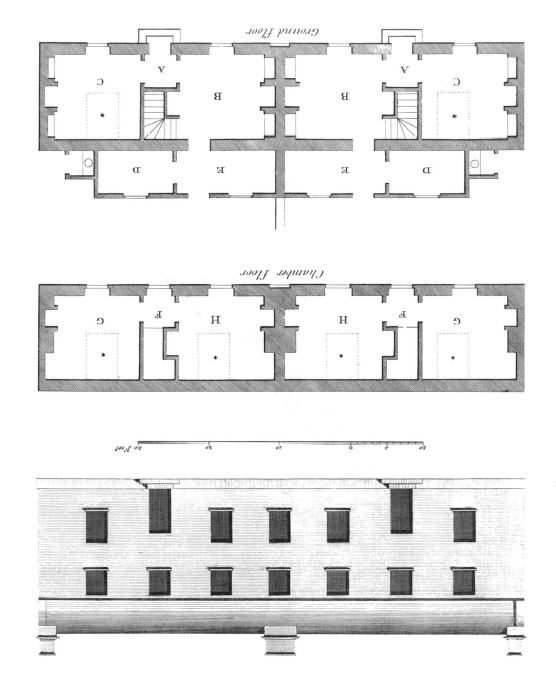

Ground Floor

Chamber Floor